MINIMALIST INTERIORS
INTÉRIEURS MINIMALISTES
MINIMALISTISCHE INTERIEURS

MINIMALIST INTERIORS
INTÉRIEURS MINIMALISTES
MINIMALISTISCHE INTERIEURS

EVERGREEN

EVERGREEN is an imprint of

Taschen GmbH

© 2005 TASCHEN GmbH

Hohenzollernring 53, D-50672 Köln

www.taschen.com

Editor Editrice Redakteur:
Simone Schleifer

Editorial assistance Assistante d'édition Veriagsassistentin:
Marta Serrats

English translation Traduction anglaise Englische Übersetzung:
Matthew Connell

French translation Traduction française Französische Übersetzung:
Marion Westerhoff

German translation Traduction allemande Deutsche Übersetzung:
Susanne Engler

Proof reading Relecture Korrektur:
Matthew Clarke, Marie-Pierre Santamarina

Art director Direction artistique Art Direktor:
Mireia Casanovas Soley

Graphic design and layout Mise en page et maquette Graphische Gestaltung und Layout:
Diego González

Printed by Imprimé en Gedruckt durch:
Artes Gráficas Toledo. Spain

ISBN: 3-8228-4188-9

Contents   Index   Inhalt

The term minimalism has not always been used correctly, and even today it continues to cause confusion when it is used to define artistic trends, schools of thought or creative movements. The term began to be bandied about in the 1960s, when artists like Donald Judd and Robert Morris broke on to the scene. Later, in the 1990s, the British architect John Pawson published the book "Minimum", which had an enormous influence on the world of design. Considered the guru of Minimalist architecture, Pawson espoused a Zen Buddhist philosophy of detachment from belongings and rejection of the accumulation of material objects, as well as the concept of simplicity as a path toward self-liberation. He felt that Minimalism as an architectural school of thought to be elitist, due to its excessive emphasis on space – now an increasingly precious commodity.

Minimalist Interiors takes us on a far-reaching visual journey through spaces that best define this esthetic. The projects presented herein are not linked solely by minimalist concepts, but also by the way in which light exerts an influence on space; by the shapes they form to configure their interior spaces; by their design and structure, and by the characteristics of their materials. All these acquire a fundamental importance, at the expense of decor and ornamentation, and without any concessions to convenience or the evocation of superfluous emotions. This, then, is an architecture that advocates specific forms, intended to relate to their surroundings and create an identity that is an amalgam of functionality, clean lines and geometric volumes.

The key to Minimalism in architecture does not lie solely in the creation or design of simple spaces, and it need not entail applying Robert Venturi's famous epithet of "less is bore". In our materialistic society, dominated by technology and revolving around information, the most important decision involves deciphering what is truly essential to life and being able to embrace modernity with only a few carefully selected possessions.

Le terme « minimalisme » n'a pas toujours été utilisé à bon escient, surtout dans le domaine de l'architecture. Aujourd'hui encore, ce mot qui prête à confusion, est l'objet de contradictions lorsqu'il s'agit de définir un courant, une école ou une tendance créatrice. Cette expression a commencé à être véhiculée pendant les années 60, lors de l'entrée en scène d'artistes célèbres, à l'instar de Donald Judd et de Robert Morris. Plus tard, dans les années 80, l'architecte John Pawson publia le livre « Minimum » qui exerça une forte influence sur le monde du design. Considéré comme le gourou de l'architecture minimaliste, il prône une attitude zen et bouddhiste qui prêche le détachement matériel et le refus de l'accumulation des biens, la simplicité en tant que philosophie de vie et forme de libération personnelle. Se référant au minimalisme en tant que courant architectural, il l'accuse d'élitisme dû à la valeur excessive accordée à l'espace qui, de nos jours, se métamorphose toujours davantage en article de luxe.

Intérieurs minimalistes est un ouvrage qui propose un parcours visuel exhaustif au gré des plus beaux espaces résumant cette esthétique, fruit d'une époque victime des excès de la société de consommation. Les projets sélectionnés se caractérisent par leur style minimaliste. Mais aussi par la lumière et son incidence sur les volumes, par la composition des édifices et la configuration de l'espace, le design et la structure, par les textures des matériaux qui acquièrent une importance fondamentale, au détriment de toute forme de décoration ou d'ornement, sans aucune concession à la commodité ou aux évocations inutiles. Une architecture, en somme, qui plaide en faveur des formes concrètes, conçues pour établir un lien avec l'environnement, et dont l'identité se définit par la fonctionnalité, la pureté des lignes et les formes géométriques.

La clé du minimalisme architectural ne réside pas uniquement dans la création et la conception d'espaces simples : il ne s'agit pas d'appliquer la célèbre expression lancée par Robert Venturi « less is bore » (moins c'est monotone). Dans une société matérialiste, basée sur l'information et dominée par la technologie, le choix fondamental à faire est de décider ce qui est vraiment essentiel pour vivre et d'être capables d'embrasser la modernité avec sa mise en valeur de certains biens soigneusement sélectionnés.

Der Begriff Minimalismus wird nicht immer korrekt verwendet, vor allem nicht in der Architektur. Auch heute noch wirft er Verwirrung und Widersprüche auf, die entstehen, wenn man damit eine Strömung, eine Schule oder einen kreativen Trend definieren möchte. Der Ausdruck kam in den Sechzigerjahren des 19. Jh. auf, als Künstler wie Donald Judd und Robert Morris allmählich bekannt wurden. In den Achtzigerjahren veröffentlichte der britische Architekt John Pawson ein Buch mit dem Titel „Minimum", das die Welt des Designs stark beeinflusste. Er wird als der Guru der minimalistischen Architektur angesehen, seine Darlegungen lassen seine vom Zen-Buddhismus beeinflusste Haltung erkennen. Die Einfachheit wird zur Lebensphilosophie und zu einer Art individueller Befreiung. Wenn man nun vom Minimalismus als eine Strömung in der Architektur spricht, wird er als elitär bezeichnet, da dem freien Raum sehr viel Wert beigemessen wird. Und freier Raum wird in der heutigen Zeit immer mehr zum Luxusartikel.

Minimalistische Interieurs lädt uns zu einem intensiven visuellen Spaziergang durch die schönsten Räume ein, in denen diese Ästhetik umgesetzt wurde, Ergebnis einer Epoche, die ein Opfer der Exzesse der Konsumgesellschaft ist. Die ausgewählten Räume sind vom minimalistischen Stil gekennzeichnet, aber auch von dem Faktor Licht und seiner Einwirkung auf die Gestaltung, von den Texturen der Materialien, die eine grundlegende Bedeutung haben und wichtiger sind als die Dekoration und Verzierungen, ohne dass dabei Komfort verloren geht oder unnötige Stilelemente verwendet werden. Man kann also von einer Architektur sprechen, die auf konkrete Formen setzt, die so entworfen sind, dass sie mit ihrer Umgebung in Beziehung stehen und deren Identität von ihrer Funktion, der Reinheit der Linien und den geometrischen Formen definiert wird.

Der Schlüssel zum architektonischen Minimalismus ist nicht nur die Erschaffung und Gestaltung von einfachen Räumen und es geht auch nicht nur darum, den berühmten Ausspruch von Robert Venturi "Less is bore" (weniger ist langweilig) umzusetzen. In einer materialistischen Gesellschaft, die auf Information beruht und von der Technologie beherrscht wird, ist die wichtigste Entscheidung die, festzulegen, was wirklich wichtig für das Leben ist und die Fähigkeit zu besitzen, sich die Modernität mit wenig, aber sorgfältig ausgewählten Dingen zu Eigen zu machen.

Private Interiors
Intérieurs privés
Private Interieurs

Apartment on Central Park
Appartement à Central Park
Appartement im Central Park

New York, USA

This spacious apartment, with breathtaking views of Central Park consists of a master bedroom, complemented by a dressing room and bathroom; an immense living room; a kitchen, dining room and large terrace, reached via a stone platform that runs the length of the apartment. There is also a meditation room, a sauna and an office. The house was furnished with pieces created by the Bonetti/Kozerski studio. The walls are finished in ivory-colored Venetian stucco, which blends well with the house's warm décor, as exemplified by the untreated teak in the dining room and master bedroom. The lighting was designed by Arnold Chan, from London's Isometrix studio, who regularly collaborates with these architects.

Cet appartement spacieux offre des vues magnifiques sur Central Park. Le projet comporte une chambre principale avec une salle de bains et un dressing attenants, un grand salon, une cuisine, une salle à manger et une large terrasse. On y accède par une plate-forme de pierre parcourant l'appartement. A cet ensemble, s'ajoutent une pièce pour méditer, un sauna et un bureau. L'habitation est meublée d'œuvres créées par le studio Bonetti/Kozerski. Le crépi des murs est en stuc vénitien couleur ivoire, en parfaite harmonie avec le choix de matériaux chaleureux pour l'intérieur, à l'instar du teck naturel de la salle à manger et de la chambre principale. L'éclairage est signé Arnold Chan, du studio londonien Isometrix, collaborant habituellement avec ces architectes.

Von dieser geräumigen Wohnung aus hat man einen wundervollen Blick auf den Central Park. Sie besteht aus einem großen Schlafzimmer, in dem sich ein Ankleideraum und ein Bad befinden, einem geräumigen Wohnzimmer, einer Küche, einem Esszimmer und einer großen Terrasse, die man über eine Steinplattform betritt, die an der Wohnung entlang verläuft. Es gibt auch einen Meditationsraum, eine Sauna und ein Büro. Die Wohnung wurde mit Möbeln des Studios Bonetti/Kozerski möbliert. Die Wände sind mit marmorfarbenem, venezianischem Stuck verkleidet, der gut zu den warmen Materialien des Hauses, wie dem Teakholz im Speisezimmer und Schlafzimmer passt. Die Beleuchtung ist ein Entwurf von Arnold Chan des Londoner Studios Isometrix. Chan arbeitet oft mit diesen Architekten zusammen.

The contrast between the teak and the ivory color of the walls and ceiling gives rise to rationalized and structured interiors.

Le contraste entre le teck, le stuc couleur ivoire des murs et le toit crée des intérieurs rationnels et structurés.

Den Kontrast zu dem Teakholz und den marmorfarbenen Wänden und Decken bildet die rationalistische und strukturierte Raumgestaltung.

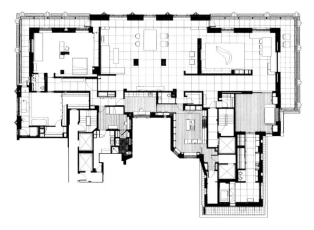

› Plan Plan Grundriss

House in Huete
Habitation à Huete
Haus in Huete

Cuenca, Spain

This house is located in a magnificent, open, untarnished natural space that had a decisive influence on its design; the result is a building with linear shapes and sophisticated finishing. The various zones of the house stretch along the length of the structure. The communal area is made up of an elongated space divided by a wooden wall, though an opening was cut into the divider to guarantee visual continuity between the two rooms. The materials used in each room reflect its function: the walls and stucco play a structural role, while the wooden partitions lend an intimate and comfortable atmosphere to the house. On the highest level of the house, the high ceilings create a bright space that enjoys ample light all year round.

La construction est implantée au cœur d'un paysage magnifique offrant un espace dégagé en pleine nature, source d'inspiration directe du projet et de sa réalisation. Il en résulte un édifice aux formes linéaires et aux finitions merveilleuses. Les zones d'utilisation sont réparties à l'intérieur et recouvrent la structure entière dans toute sa longueur. L'aire commune prend la forme d'un espace allongé divisé par un mur en bois pourvu d'une ouverture pour assurer le lien visuel entre les zones de vie. Les matériaux employés définissent la fonction de chaque pièce : les murs, recouverts de stuc, ont une fonction structurelle et les cloisons de bois confèrent à l'espace une ambiance intime et confortable. Dans les parties hautes de la construction, les toits anciens ont permis de concevoir un espace diaphane parfaitement éclairé.

Dieses Haus befindet sich in einer wundervollen Umgebung, auf einem freien Platz mitten in der Natur. Diese Umgebung hat die Planung und Ausführung deutlich beeinflusst, so dass ein Gebäude mit linearen Formen und edlen Materialien entstanden ist. Die Nutzflächen im Inneren verteilen sich über die gesamte Struktur. Der gemeinsame Wohnbereich besteht aus einem länglichen Raum, der von einer Holzwand geteilt wird, in der eine Öffnung eine visuelle Verbindung zwischen den Räumen schafft. Die Materialien definieren die Funktion jedes Raumes, die Wände mit Stuck gehören zur Struktur, während die Raumteiler aus Holz für eine intime und komfortable Wohnumgebung sorgen. Im doersten Bereich des Hauses mit seinen hohen Decken entstand ein Raum, der perfekt beleuchtet ist.

The design of the exterior displays an extreme purity and consistency.

Le dessin des lignes extérieures de l'édifice en exalte l'extrême pureté.

Die äußere Gestaltung des Gebäudes ist sehr rein und konsistent.

Like the other rooms, the bathroom expresses its identity through linear forms and purity of materials.

A l'instar des autres pièces, la salle de bains se définit par ses formes linéaires et par la pureté des matériaux.

Wie auch die anderen Räume ist das Bad von linearen Formen und der Reinheit der Materialien gekennzeichnet.

Kamakura House
Maison Kamakura
Haus Kamakura

Kamakura, Japan

This project is located on the road that leading to Mount Kamakura, on a lot previously occupied by a neighbor's garden. A flat, one-story volume situated behind a garden endows this site with a degree of depth characteristic of the surrounding urban area. A second, two-story volume is fitted under a sloping roof. So as to make this three-dimensional space more attractive, the various levels were connected with delicate stairways that allow its inhabitants to roam freely. The result is a compact house that appears to be far more spacious than it actually is. The small terrace situated on the roof offers picturesque night-time views of the mountains in the distance.

Ce projet est situé sur la route qui conduit au col de la montagne Kamakura. La maison est actuellement implantée à l'endroit où se trouvait le jardin de l'habitation voisine. Un volume plat d'un seul niveau, doté d'un jardin à l'avant, confère au lieu une profondeur caractéristique de l'ensemble du paysage environnant. Un autre volume, sur deux hauteurs, se love sous une toiture inclinée. Pour accroître l'attrait de cet espace tridimensionnel, les niveaux différents sont reliés entre eux par de fins escaliers, permettant aux habitants de se déplacer dans toute la maison. Cette conception offre un habitat compact donnant l'impression d'être plus spacieux qu'il ne l'est en réalité. La petite terrasse, insérée dans le toit, offre des vues nocturnes pittoresques avec les montagnes en toile de fond.

Dieses Haus steht an dem Weg zum Berg Kamakura. Auf dem Grundstück befand sich vorher der Garten des Nachbarhauses. Ein flaches, einstöckiges Gebäude mit einem Vorgarten gibt dem Ort eine Tiefe, die das gemeinsame Kennzeichen der umgebenden Stadtlandschaft ist. Ein anderes, zweistöckiges Gebäude ist mit einem geneigten Dach gedeckt. Um diesen dreidimensionalen Raum zu verschönern, wurden die verschiedenen Ebenen mit zierlichen Treppen verbunden, über die sich die Bewohner durch das ganze Haus bewegen können. So entstand ein kompaktes Haus, das den Eindruck erweckt, größer zu sein als es wirklich ist. Von der kleinen Dachterrasse aus hat man vor allem nachts einen wundervollen Blick mit den Bergen als Hintergrund.

The architect designed the house so that the slope of the main roof would not hinder the growth of a cherry tree in the garden.

L'architecte a conçu la maison de sorte que le degré d'inclinaison de la toiture principale ne gêne pas le cerisier du jardin.

Der Architekt entwarf das Haus so, dass die Neigung des Daches nicht den Wachstum des Kirschbaums im Garten behindert.

Similar materials were used in the kitchen and bathroom to unify the textures and colors of the finishes.

Des matériaux identiques sont employés dans la cuisine et la salle de bains pour unifier les textures et les teintes des finitions.

In Küche und Bad wurden ähnliche Materialien verwendet, um die Texturen und Töne zu vereinheitlichen.

Hakuei Residence
Résidence Hakuei
Haus Hakuei

Osaka, Japan

The site of this house is delimited by the intersection of two streets, and the basic concept behind its design stemmed from the idea of visually connecting the exterior with the interior. Discontinuous walls were used to distribute the interior spaces and achieve fluidity and continuity. The house was designed in keeping with the premises of Minimalism: theatrical treatment of lighting, noble materials, simplicity of forms and rational arrangement of elements are just some of the details that testify to the efficiency and elegance underlying this design. The courtyard echoes the lightweight structures of the interior and reinforces the relationship between the two through a high degree of spatial continuity. The tree located in the center of the courtyard represents a point of synthesis between the cycles of nature, life, and the passing of time.

Deux rues qui s'entrecroisent, délimitent le terrain où se trouve cette maison. La conception de base du plan est partie de l'idée de relier visuellement l'extérieur avec l'intérieur. La distribution de l'espace se fait grâce à des murs ouverts, lui conférant fluidité et continuité. La maison a été construite selon les critères minimalistes : la mise en scène théâtrale de l'éclairage, la noblesse des matériaux, la simplicité des formes et la disposition rationnelle des éléments sont certains des détails montrant que nous sommes devant un projet alliant efficacité et élégance. Le patio reproduit la légèreté structurelle de l'intérieur renforçant la relation et la continuité spatiale. L'arbre, au centre du patio, est la synthèse entre les cycles de la nature, la vie et le temps qui passe.

Das Grundstück, auf dem dieses Haus steht, wird von zwei sich überschneidenden Straßen begrenzt. Das grundlegende Konzept der Gestaltung ging von der Idee aus, das Äußere visuell mit dem Inneren zu verbinden. Um den Raum zu unterteilen, wurden unterbrochene Wände benutzt, die einen Eindruck von Fließen und Kontinuität vermitteln. Das Haus wurde nach minimalistischen Gesichtspunkten gestaltet. Die Beleuchtung ist sehr theatralisch und die Aufteilung der Elemente rational. So entstand ein Gebäude, das funktionell und zugleich elegant ist. Im Hof wurde die strukturelle Leichtigkeit der Räume wiederholt und die Beziehung zum Raum und die Kontinuität unterstrichen. Der Baum in der Mitte des Hofes symbolisiert die Synthese zwischen den Zyklen der Natur, dem Leben und dem Fortschreiten der Zeit.

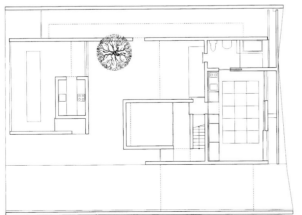

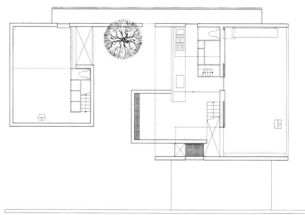

› Plans Plans Grundrisse

House without walls
Maison sans murs
Haus ohne Wände

Nagano, Japan

This pavilion forms part of a series of experimental projects described by their architect as "One-off Houses". The fundamental idea behind this project was to establish spatial continuity between the interior and the exterior. Delimiting factors were therefore eliminated: the interior is entirely free of partitions, and the bathroom is open to view, in the middle of this open ensemble. Only in the kitchen, the benches and odd pieces of furniture convey the feeling of a differentiated space, although this does not affect the homogeneity of the space. The interior incorporates moveable panels that allow for a range of possibilities as regards the layout of the house, in addition to changing its personality. The curved lines of the structure are so simple that the walls seem to cease to exist, making the house blend completely into the landscape.

Ce pavillon fait partie d'une série de projets expérimentaux que l'architecte appelle « Monographies de Maisons ». L'idée essentielle de ce projet est d'établir une continuité spatiale entre l'intérieur et l'extérieur sans entrave spatiale : l'espace intérieur est dépourvu de cloisons et la salle de bains est visible au cœur de l'ensemble ouvert. Dans la cuisine uniquement, les bancs et certains éléments du mobilier suggèrent que nous sommes dans une zone différente, ce qui, d'ailleurs, n'affecte en rien le caractère homogène de l'espace. L'intérieur intègre des panneaux mobiles qui permettent de moduler la distribution de l'espace, lui conférant ainsi un nouveau caractère. Les lignes tout en courbes de la structure sont si simples que les murs semblent inexistants et donnent l'impression que la maison fait partie du paysage.

Dieser Pavillon gehört zu einer Reihe experimenteller Projekte, die der Architekt als „Häuser-Monographie" bezeichnet. Die grundlegende Idee war es, eine räumliche Kontinuität zwischen außen und innen zu entwickeln. Begrenzungen wurden entfernt. Der Innenraum hat keine Raumteiler und das Bad ist mitten in dem offenen Raum zu sehen. Nur die Küche, die Bänke und einige Möbelstücke zeigen uns, dass wir uns in einem bestimmten Bereich befinden, was jedoch die einheitliche Gestaltung des Raumes nicht negativ beeinflusst. Im Inneren gibt es verschiebbare Wände, mit denen man den Raum auf verschiedene Weise aufteilen und verändern kann. Die kurvigen Formen der Struktur sind so einfach, dass die Wände nicht zu existieren scheinen und man gewinnt den Eindruck, dass das Haus zur Landschaft gehört.

The daring concept behind this project challenges functionality and lays a theoretical groundwork that can be used by other architects.

Le concept audacieux de ce projet est un défi à la fonctionnalité. Il pose des bases théoriques qui peuvent servir de modèles à d'autres architectes.

Dieses gewagte Konzept stellt nicht nur eine Herausforderung an die Funktionalität dar, sondern schafft theoretische Grundlagen, die von anderen Architekten genutzt werden können.

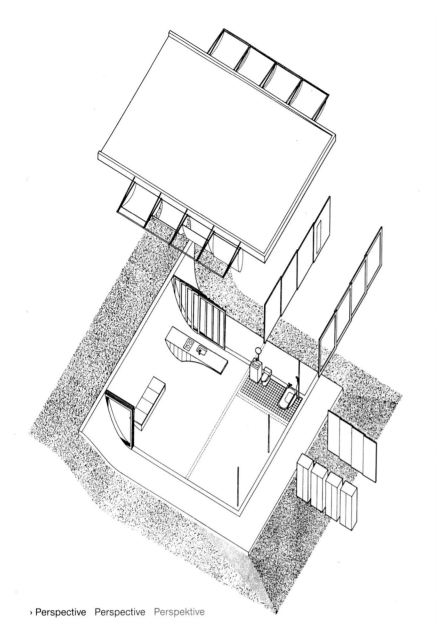

› Perspective   Perspective   Perspektive

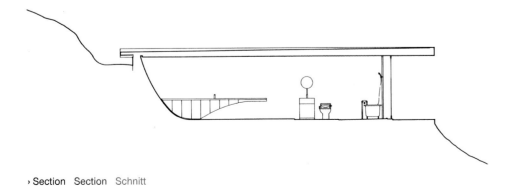

› Section   Section   Schnitt

› Plan   Plan   Grundiss

The design reveals the architects' desire not to influence the house's surroundings. The alterations are minimal: the house seems not even to occupy the site it sits on.

Le concept révèle l'intention des architectes de sauvegarder l'environnement. L'impact sur la nature est minime donnant l'impression que la maison n'occupe pas l'espace.

Die Architekten wollten bei der Gestaltung nicht in die Umgebung eingreifen. Es wurde kaum etwas verändert und das Haus fügt sich harmonisch in die Landschaft ein.

Ciatti House
Maison Ciatti
Haus Ciatti

Florence, Italy

This austere house, built with materials typical of the area, rises from the Tuscan landscape. The project revolves around the creation of double-height central nuclei flooded by light pouring in through skylights. These symmetrical openings were strategically designed to favor the illumination of the rooms, which are spread over two levels. The lower level contains the living room, kitchen and reading area, while the first floor holds the bedrooms, bathroom and another living room. The architect wanted to reinterpret the traditional materials of the region and use them to accentuate the voids, lighting and shadows; likewise, for the structural elements, he opted for natural materials like limestone and wood.

Cette habitation austère, construite dans les matériaux typiques de la région, s'élève au cœur du paysage toscan. Le projet se base sur la création de noyaux centraux à double hauteur, bénéficiant au maximum de la lumière naturelle qui pénètre par les velux. La conception de ces ouvertures symétriques permet de favoriser l'éclairage des pièces à vivre qui s'articulent sur deux niveaux. Le rez-de-chaussée héberge le salon, la cuisine et une zone de lecture, alors que le premier niveau abrite les chambres, la salle de bains et un autre salon. L'architecte a voulu mettre en scène les matériaux typiques de la région afin d'accentuer les vides, l'éclairage et les ombres. En ce qui concerne les éléments structuraux il a opté pour des matériaux naturels comme la pierre calcaire et le bois.

Dieses schlichte Wohnhaus aus typischen Materialien der Region steht mitten in der Toskana. Es wurden zentrale Kernstücke doppelter Höhe geschaffen, in die durch Fensterluken reichlich Tageslicht einfällt. Diese symmetrischen Öffnungen sind strategisch so verteilt, dass die Räume auf den beiden Stockwerken Licht erhalten. Im Erdgeschoss befinden sich das Wohnzimmer, die Küche und ein Lesebereich, im ersten Stock die Schlafzimmer, das Bad und ein zweiter Wohnbereich. Der Architekt wollte die typischen Materialien der Region neu interpretieren und mit ihnen die Leere, die Beleuchtung und die Schatten unterstreichen. Die strukturellen Elemente sind aus natürlichen Materialien wie Kalkstein und Holz.

The use of skylights allows an abundant amount of natural light to enter the house and emphasizes the simplicity of the structure.

Les lucarnes de toit permettent à la lumière naturelle d'entrer à flots et rehaussent la simplicité de la structure.

Die Dachfenster lassen reichlich Tageslicht in die Räume einfallen und unterstreichen die Einfachheit der Struktur.

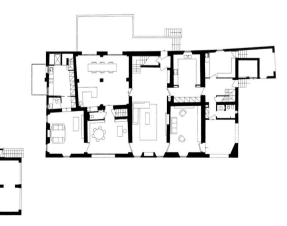

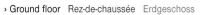

› Ground floor Rez-de-chaussée Erdgeschoss

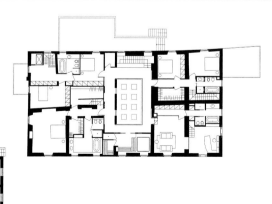

› First floor Premier étage Erstes Obergeschoss

In this space – where stainless steel rubs shoulders with clay-tile vaulting in the ceiling – the combination of contemporary elements with other, more traditional materials is evident.

L'alliance d'éléments contemporains et d'autres plus traditionnels est sublimée au cœur de cet espace où l'acier inoxydable cohabite avec les tuiles de la voûte du toit.

Durch die Kombination von zeitgenössischen Elementen und traditionellen gewinnt der Raum, in dem Edelstahl mit einer Kuppel aus Ziegelstein kombiniert ist, an Wirkung.

Yutenji T House
Habitation Yutenji T
Haus Yutenji T

Tokyo, Japan

The Yutenji T House is located on a hill in the Setagaya neighborhood. The building, which is deeper than its façade would seem to suggest, faces toward a busy motorway to the east. The architect took as his inspiration the owners' working methods, so he designed the type of space he felt would best suit their lifestyle. The upper floor of the house contains a living room and a workshop. The boundary between the interior and the exterior of the façade is marked by translucent double-glazing. The appearance of each space in the house varies according to the angle from which it is viewed and the intensity of the natural light. Far from designing projects and coordinating interiors, Toyo Ito aims to capture the imaginative world of a house's inhabitants and anticipate how they will react to or interpret a space.

La maison Yutenji T est située sur la cime d'une colline du quartier de Setagaya. L'édifice, d'une profondeur supérieure à ce que la façade laisse à supposer, oriente sa face est vers une artère fréquentée de la ville. L'architecte s'est inspiré de la méthode de travail des propriétaires pour imaginer l'espace le mieux adapté à leur style de vie. L'étage supérieur de la maison héberge le salon et un atelier. La limite entre l'intérieur et l'extérieur de la façade est soulignée par une vitre à double vitrage translucide. L'aspect de chacun des espaces de la maison varie en fonction de la perception visuelle des habitants et de l'intensité de la lumière naturelle. Plus que de concevoir des projets et d'agencer des intérieurs, Toyo Ito tente de saisir l'imaginaire de ses habitants, leur perception et interprétation personnelles de l'espace.

Das Haus Yutenji T steht oben auf einem Hügel im Viertel Setagaya. Das Gebäude ist tiefer, als die Fassade glauben macht, und die Ostseite liegt an einer stark befahrenden Straße der Stadt. Der Architekt ließ sich von der Arbeitsmethodologie der Eigentümer inspirieren, um einen Raum zu schaffen, der sich optimal an deren Lebensstil anpasst. Im oberen Stockwerk befinden sich das Wohnzimmer und eine Werkstatt. Die Begrenzung zwischen Innen und Außen bildet eine lichtdurchlässige, doppelte Glasscheibe. Das Aussehen der Räume ändert sich je nach Blickwinkel der Bewohner und Intensität des Tageslichtes. Toyo Ito ging es nicht darum, ein Projekt zu entwerfen und die Räume zu koordinieren, sondern die Empfindungen der Bewohner einzufangen und deren Gefühle und Interpretation der Räume umzusetzen.

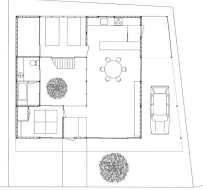

› Plan Plan Grundriss

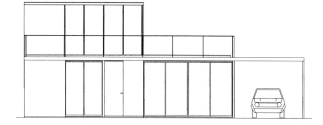

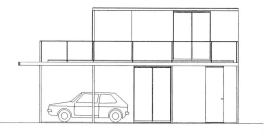

› Sections Sections Schnitte

White loft
Loft Blanc
Weißes Loft

London, UK

This apartment, conceived as a single environment, is white throughout and permeable to whatever light that makes its way in. The space is fluid and uninterrupted, eliminating any elements that would enclose spaces or present visual barriers – the bedroom is the only room separated from the rest, by means of a series of opaque methacrylate panels. Rotating on an axis, the panels form a filter for the light coming in, allowing it to establish different relationships with the other spaces in the house. The kitchen stands out on account of its extreme Minimalism: it is a block sculpted from brilliantly-colored wood varnished in red lacquer that is reflected by the resin floors. In contrast with the clean lines of the house, the exposed brick wall in the dining room harks back to previous incarnations of the apartment. The result is a loft that is both ethereal and subtle, with light as clearly the most important player.

Cet appartement, conçu à l'instar d'un univers unique, est entièrement blanc et perméable a la lumière. L'espace est fluide et continu, dépourvu d'éléments de fermeture ou de barrières visuelles, la chambre étant le seul espace séparé des autres par une série de cloisons en méthacrylate opaque. Pivotant sur leur axe, les cloisons filtrent la lumière, établissant différentes relations avec le reste de l'intérieur. La cuisine se démarque par un minimalisme porté à l'extrême : un bloc sculpté dans le bois, laqué de rouge, illumine l'espace et se reflète dans le carrelage en résine. Contrastant avec la pureté des lignes de la maison, le mur en briques apparentes de la salle à manger n'est pas sans rappeler l'appartement antérieur. Il en résulte un loft éthéré et subtil où la lumière est le protagoniste de l'espace.

Diese Wohnung wurde als ein einziger Raum angelegt, ganz in Weiß und lichtdurchlässig. Es gibt keine schließenden Elemente oder visuelle Barrieren. Nur das Schlafzimmer ist vom übrigen Raum durch eine Reihe von Paneelen aus undurchsichtigem Metacrylat abgetrennt. Wenn man die Paneele über ihre Achse dreht, bilden sie einen Lichtfilter, durch den verschiedene Beziehungen mit dem übrigen Raum entstehen können. In der Küche wurde der Minimalismus auf extremste Weise umgesetzt, ein aus rotlackiertem Holz geschnitzter Block glänzt in dem Raum und wird von dem Kunstharzfußboden reflektiert. Im Gegensatz zu den reinen Linien des Hauses erinnern die unverputzten Mauern im Esszimmer an das frühere Aussehen des Lofts. Entstanden ist ein ätherisches und subtiles Loft, in dem das Element Licht die Hauptrolle spielt.

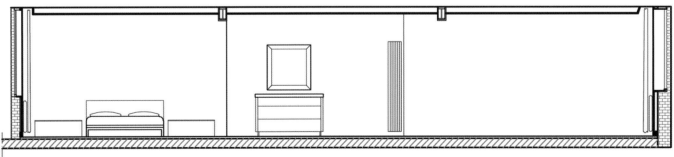

› **Section** Section Schnitt

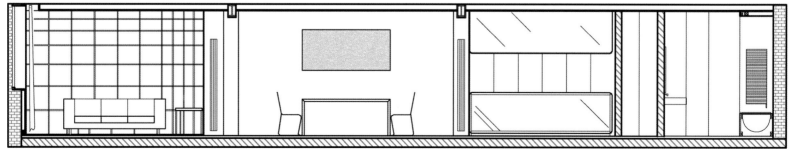

› Section   Section   Schnitt

K House
Maison K
Haus K

Tokyo, Japan

Here, the architects of the K House designed a solid structure that would serve as the skeleton for the walls that would hold up the building; in order to achieve this, they built a reinforced structure with seven-inch-thick walls and a single reinforcement at ground level. The project was defined as a "shelf structure", as it appears to reorganize the various spaces as though they were shelves attached to the walls. A metal stairway leads to the last and highest "shelf", which houses a bathtub deliberately located under one of the main skylights: the beam of light that illuminates it perpendicularly enhances the prominent role it plays in the esthetics of the upper level of the dwelling. This shelf also stands out for its distinctive red armchair, which adds a splash of color to an otherwise neutral and relaxed environment.

Les architectes ont conçu une structure solide servant d'arrête aux murs qui soutiennent l'édifice. Pour y parvenir, ils ont créé une armature renforcée avec des murs de 18 cm de large et une base unique de soutient. Le projet porte le nom de « structure d'étagères », car il donne l'impression de réorganiser les différents espaces à l'image d'un rayonnage fixé dans le mur. Un escalier métallique mène au dernier étage, le plus élevé, où une baignoire est installée exprès sous l'une des lucarnes principales. L'éclairage perpendiculaire du faisceau lumineux met en relief le papier remarquable, point d'orgue esthétique du niveau supérieur de l'habitation. A cet étage, un fauteuil rouge se détache également, ajoutant une touche de couleur à un univers neutre et détendu.

Die Architekten entwarfen eine solide Struktur, die als Basis für die Wände dient, die das Gebäude stützen. Dazu wurde ein 18 cm breites, festes Gerust mit Wänden und einer einzigen Verstärkung entworfen. Das Projekt wurde als „Regalstruktur" definiert, da die verschiedenen Räume so organisiert sind, als ob es sich um an den Wänden befestigte Regalbretter handelt. Eine Metalltreppe führt bis zum letzten und höchsten Regal, wo sich eine Badewanne unter dem Hauptdachfenster befindet. Der Lichtstrahl, der sie senkrecht von oben beleuchtet, unterstreicht die wichtige Rolle, die die Ästhetik im obersten Geschoss der Wohnung spielt. Auf diesem Regal fällt auch ein roter Sessel ins Auge, der der neutralen und entspannenden Umgebung einen Pinselstrich Farbe hinzufügt.

A series of metal stairs lead to the various levels, all the way up to the top – which is situated beneath the roof.

Des escaliers métalliques permettent d'accéder aux niveaux différents jusqu'au dernier plan, situé sous le toit.

Über die Metalltreppen erreicht man die verschiedenen Ebenen bis zum letzten Regal direkt unter dem Dach.

Residence in Nagoya
Résidence en Nagoya
Haus in Nagoya

Nagoya, Japan

Starting from the idea of establishing a dialogue between private and public spaces, the design of this house entailed a system of five circles arranged transversally between the walls of the structure. The front part of each circle houses a private room, such as the bedrooms or the children's play area, while the rear areas are reserved for bathrooms or living rooms. This ensured that the residents would be able to move freely between the exterior and interior of each circle. The final result would have never been possible had standard connections been made between the rooms. A material that guarantees transparency and allows light to enter the house is used in some of the walls. As a result, the circles seem to form a single entity despite being on different levels.

L'idée de faire communiquer l'espace privé et l'espace public entre eux, est le point de départ de la conception d'un système de cinq cercles placé transversalement entre les murs de la structure. La partie antérieure de chaque cercle héberge une sphère de vie privée, à l'instar de chambres à coucher ou de zone ludique pour les enfants. La partie postérieure, en revanche, est réservée à la salle de bains ou à la salle de séjour. De cette façon, les habitants peuvent circuler librement de manière fluide à l'extérieur comme à l'intérieur de chaque cercle. Cela n'aurait jamais été possible sur la base d'une communication traditionnelle entre les espaces de vie. Les murs de certaines sphères utilisent un matériau à base de verre garantissant la transparence et l'éclairage intérieur. De cette façon, les cercles, disposés à des niveaux différents, semblent faire partie du même ensemble.

Grundlage des Projektes war es, dass eine Verbindung zwischen dem privaten und dem öffentlichen Bereich des Hauses hergestellt werden sollte. Deshalb entwarf man ein System aus fünf Kreisen, die quer zwischen die Wände der Struktur gelegt wurden. Der Teil vor jedem Kreis beherbergt einen privaten Raum wie die Schlafzimmer und das Kinderzimmer, und in dem Teil nach dem Kreis befinden sich das Bad und das Wohnzimmer. So wurde erreicht, dass die Bewohner sich frei im Äußeren und Inneren jedes Kreises bewegen können. Dieses Endergebnis hätte man mit einer klassischen Verbindung der Räume nicht erreicht. An einigen Wänden wurde ein glasartiges Material benutzt, so dass sie transparent sind und Tageslicht ins Innere fällt. Die Kreise, die auf verschiedenen Ebenen angelegt sind, scheinen eine einzige Gruppe zu bilden.

In the middle of the space, the onlooker's attention is drawn by five circles, located randomly between the walls; these contain the private rooms.

Au cœur de l'espace, cinq cercles se détachent, placés au hasard entre les murs, abritant chacun les sphères privées.

Mitten im Raum heben sich fünf Kreise ab, die sich wie zufällig zwischen den Wänden zu befinden scheinen. Dort liegen die privaten Räume.

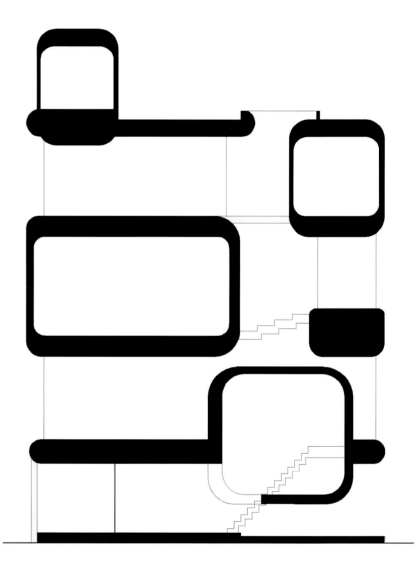

› Section Section Schnitt

Loft in Venice
Loft à Venise
Loft in Venedig

Venice, Italy

This project aimed to combine the characteristic look of an industrial space with the needs of a family. The building comprises a generous space with sixteen-foot ceilings that is predominantly painted and decorated with white. An intermediate level, which occupies nearly half the floor space, contains the night-time areas, while the remainder consists of the double-height main space, onto which the bedrooms open. Two large lacquered volumes were inserted beneath the intermediate level to cordon off the kitchen. They act as though they were containers in transit, and the spaces they create are remarkably ephemeral in nature. One of them serves as the guest bedroom and is entirely surrounded by glass walls, while the other serves as a service area that doubles into a photography darkroom. Through a precise distribution of spaces, privacy has been happily married with flexibility.

Ce projet cherche à associer l'expression typique d'un espace industriel aux besoins d'une famille. L'édifice est composé d'un volume généreux de 5 m de haut où le blanc est la couleur dominante. Un entresol, occupant presque la moitié de l'étage, abrite la zone de nuit avec les chambres à coucher qui donnent sur la partie restante, accueillant l'espace principal sur deux hauteurs. Deux grands volumes laqués, séparant la zone de la cuisine, ont été insérés sous l'entresol, à l'instar de containers temporaires, soulignant le côté éphémère de leurs espaces respectifs. L'un d'eux abrite la chambre d'amis, espace entièrement vitré; l'autre, est une zone de service qui se transforme en laboratoire photo. Cette distribution spatiale bien étudiée, permet de conjuguer intimité et espace modulable.

Bei dieser Raumgestaltung sollte der typische Charakter einer Fabriketage den Ansprüchen einer Familie gerecht werden. Das Gebäude besteht aus fünf großen 5 Meter hohen Teilen. Vorherrschend ist die Farbe Weiß. Auf dem Zwischengeschoss, das fast die Hälfte eines Stockwerkes einnimmt, liegen die Schlafzimmer, den übrigen Teil nimmt ein Raum doppelter Höhe ein, zu dem sich die Schlafzimmer öffnen. Zwei große, lackierte Formen, die den Küchenbereich abtrennen, wurden unter dem Zwischengeschoss eingeführt. Sie zeigen, dass die jeweiligen Räume temporär eingerichtet sind und sich verändern können. Eine dieser Formen ist das völlig verglaste Gästezimmer, die andere ein Abstell- und Arbeitsraum, der zum Fotolabor werden kann. Durch die genaue Verteilung der Räume wurde Privatsphäre möglich, ohne an Flexibilität zu verlieren.

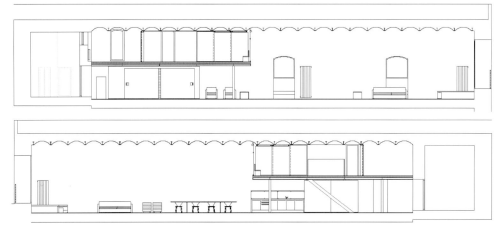

› Sections Sections Schnitte

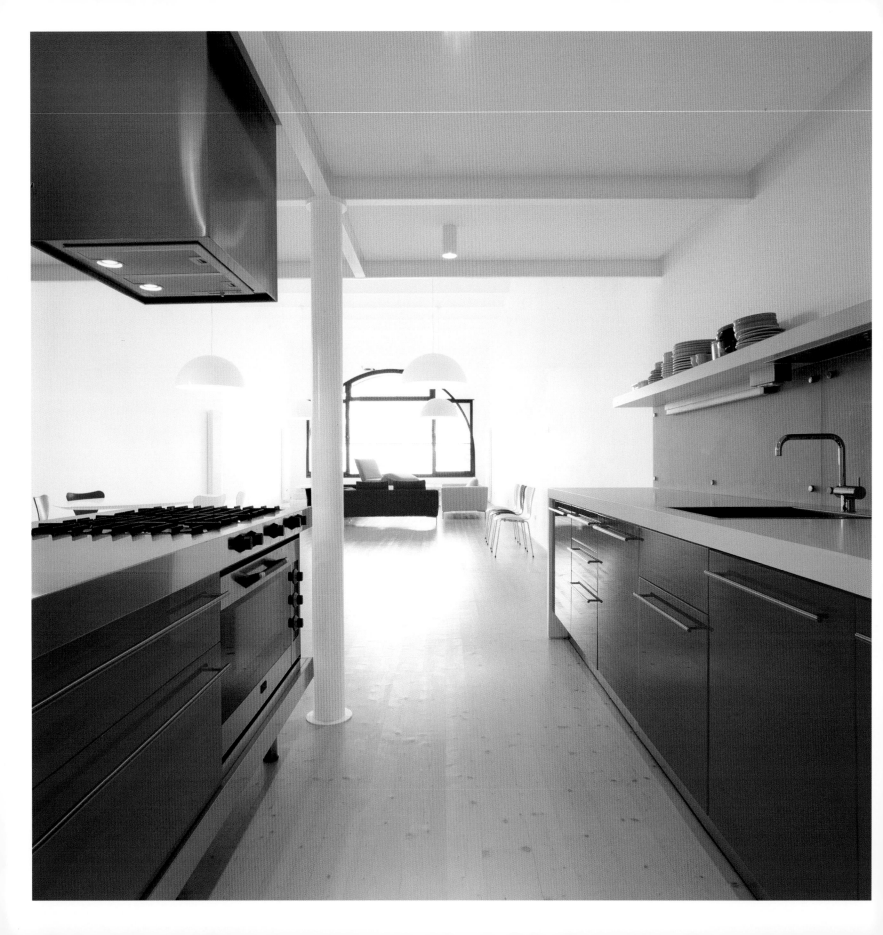

Dwelling on the Thames
Habitation au bord de la Tamise
Haus an der Themse

London, UK

The client who commissioned this house wanted it to be built in a space measuring nearly 2,000 sq. ft. on the fifth floor of an old warehouse. This irregular volume was made up of a system of circular columns and beams: a sequence of windows and dark, exposed-brick walls. A 75-foot-long wall – which separates the guest bedroom, the service area, kitchen and bathrooms from the spacious living room – is fitted with all the service installations and is interrupted at points for light to enter from the east side of the building and reach the hall. The lines drawn by the flagstones on the floor reinforce the geometry of the wall that organizes the space, while the closet focuses attention toward the living room. The end of the wall transforms into the headboard of the bed in the master bedroom –a room that can be opened or closed with respect to the living room by means of a thirteen-foot-long sliding door.

Le client a acquis un container de 185 m² au cinquième étage d'un ancien magasin. Le volume, de forme irrégulière, est constitué d'un système de colonnes circulaires et de poutres, d'une enfilade de fenêtres et de murs sombres en briques apparentes. Un mur de 23 m de long, qui sépare la chambre d'amis, les services, la cuisine et les salles de bains du grand salon, héberge toutes les installations et n'est interrompu que par des ouvertures qui permettent à la lumière de l'est de pénétrer la zone d'entrée. Le réticule dessiné par l'assemblage du carrelage de pierre souligne la géométrie organisatrice de l'espace mural. Le meuble constituant le vestiaire est un point d'orgue qui mène au salon. Le mur s'achève en formant la tête du lit de la chambre principal, espace qui peut s'ouvrir ou se fermer à volonté vers le salon, par le biais d'une porte coulissante de quatre mètres.

Der Kunde kaufte eine 185 m² große Fläche im fünften Stock eines ehemaligen Lagerhauses. Das unregelmäßig geformte Gebäude besteht aus einem System kreisförmiger Säulen und Träger, einer zweiten Sequenz Fenster und dunklen, unverputzten Ziegelwänden. Eine 23 Meter lange Wand trennt das Gästezimmer, den Waschraum, die Küche und die Bäder vom Wohnzimmer. In dieser Wand sind alle Installationen untergebracht und sie ist unterbrochen, damit das Licht, das vom Osten kommt, den Eingangsbereich erreicht. Das Raster, das die Fugen des Bodenbelags aus Stein zeichnen, unterstreicht die organisierende Geometrie des Raumes der Mauer. Das Möbelstück zum Aufbewahren der Kleider lenkt die Aufmerksamkeit auf das Wohnzimmer. Das Ende der Wand wird zum Kopfteil des Bettes im Hauptschlafzimmer. Dieses Zimmer kann man nach Belieben mit einer vier Meter langen Schiebetür zum Wohnzimmer hin öffnen oder schließen.

The 75-foot-long wall organizes the spaces in the house and acts as a counterpoint to its irregular forms.

Le mur, de 23 mètres de long, agence l'espace et s'affiche en contrepoint à l'irrégularité formelle de la maison.

Die 23 m lange Mauer ordnet den Raum und bildet den Kontrapunkt zu den unregelmäßigen Formen der Wohnung.

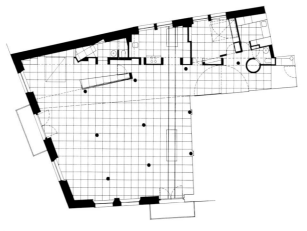

› Plan   Plan   Grundriss

Malvern House
Maison Malvern
Haus Malvern

Melbourne, Australia

This house in Melbourne was built in 1930 and renovated in 1960 with the addition of a new wing and significant changes to the interior. A more recent refurbishment involved the modernization of the entire house and a radical redistribution of its spaces. This renovation focused on the rear section of the dwelling – the busiest part of the house – which now enjoys an extremely well-positioned garden. The transformation of the former kitchen into a studio marks the transition between the newer and older parts of the house. In addition to changes in program, the house – originally very dark – was fully opened up to natural light via the opening of a series of skylights, so the new studio was totally integrated into the newer part of the building. The third bedroom is also part of this expansion; it is open to light pouring in from the garden through a window, which is made of frosted glass to protect the occupants' privacy.

Cette maison de Melbourne, construite en 1930, a été restaurée en 1960, lui ajoutant une nouvelle aile avec d'importantes modifications intérieures. La dernière étape de la restauration, consacrée à la modernisation de toute la maison, en a changé radicalement la distribution. La rénovation a modifié essentiellement la partie arrière de l'habitation, où se déroule la plus grande partie des activités, agrémentée aujourd'hui d'un jardin très bien orienté. La transformation de l'ancienne cuisine en un studio marque le passage entre la partie ancienne et la nouvelle. Au changement des fonctions, s'ajoute l'apport de lumière naturelle au cœur de la maison grâce à l'installation de velux : l'ancienne cuisine est ainsi parfaitement intégrée à la nouvelle construction. La troisième chambre à coucher est également comprise dans cet agrandissement. Elle reçoit la lumière du jardin à travers une vitre dont le verre est légèrement opaque pour préserver l'intimité.

Dieses Haus in Melbourne wurde 1930 errichtet und 1960 renoviert. Außerdem wurde ein neuer Flügel angebaut und die Räume stark verändert. Der letzte Eingriff war die Modernisierung des ganzen Hauses mit einer radikalen Veränderung der Raumeinteilung. Die Renovierung konzentrierte sich auf den hinteren Teil des Hauses, wo die meisten Aktivitäten stattfinden und wo sich ein schön gelegener Garten befindet. Die alte, zum Atelier umgebaute Küche markiert den Übergang von dem alten Teil zum Neubau. Nicht nur die Aufteilung wurde verändert, sondern es gelangt auch mehr Tageslicht in die Mitte des Hauses, die vorher sehr dunkel war. Das erreichte man mithilfe von Dachfenstern. Die alte Küche wurde in den Neubau aufgenommen. Das dritte Schlafzimmer gehört auch zu dem Anbau. Hier fällt das Tageslicht aus dem Garten durch satiniertes Glas ein, so dass die Privatsphäre geschützt bleibt.

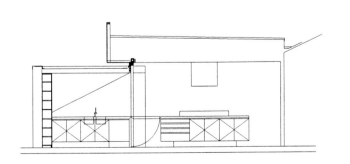 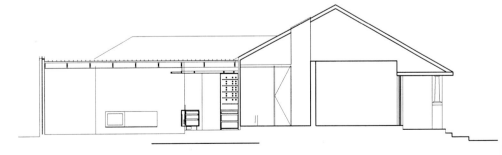

› Sections Sections Schnitte

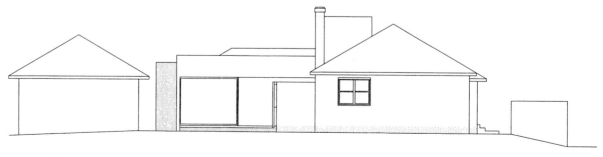

› Elevation Élévation Aufriss

Artist's residence
Résidence d'artiste
Künstlerwohnung

Beijing, China

This house was designed by artist Ai Wei Wei and serves as both his studio and home. The building's structure is reinforced concrete clad in red brick on the inside and grey brick outside, set off by large, well-proportioned windows that are mobile and open on to the various façades. The main part of the building consists of the artist's two-story studio; designed without windows, it was intended to be lit from above by two skylights in the ceiling. The artist reduced the range of materials used in the construction to an absolute minimum. In designing his personal studio, Ai Wei Wei placed special emphasis on achieving the ideal scale and proportions, as well as judicious use of the basic materials. These, according to him, represent the essential elements of architecture.

Cette maison, dessinée par l'artiste Ai Wei Wei, comprend son atelier attenant à l'espace consacré à la sphère privée. L'édifice possède une structure en béton armé, revêtue de briques rouges à l'intérieur et de briques grises, à l'extérieur. De grandes baies vitrées amovibles s'ouvrent sur les façades dans d'élégantes proportions. La partie principale de l'édifice est composée du studio à deux étages de l'artiste : dépourvu de fenêtres, il est conçu pour recevoir la lumière naturelle grâce à deux velux de toit. L'artiste a réduit au minimum l'éventail de matériaux utilisés pour la construction. Pour Ai Wei Wei, la conception de son propre studio l'a poussé à réussir une échelle et des proportions parfaites et à employer judicieusement les matériaux de base qui sont, à son avis, les éléments architecturaux essentiels.

Dieses Haus wurde von dem Künstler Ai Wei Wei entworfen und enthält ein Atelier und die Privatwohnung. Das Gebäude besitzt eine Struktur aus Stahlbeton, die innen mit rotem Ziegelstein und außen mit grauen Steinen verkleidet ist. Es befinden sich in den Fassaden große bewegliche Fenster mit eleganten Proportionen. Der Hauptteil des Hauses besteht aus einem zweistöckigen Atelier ohne Fenster. Das Tageslicht fällt durch zwei Dachfenster ein. Der Künstler verwendete äußerst wenig Materialien für den Bau. Ai Wei Wei legte beim Entwurf seines eigenen Ateliers besonderen Nachdruck auf das Erreichen einer Skala, korrekte Proportionen und den angemessenen Einsatz der grundlegenden Materialien, da dies seiner Meinung nach die wichtigsten Elemente der Architektur sind.

The studio was designed to maximize natural light and to bring out the natural beauty of the materials used throughout the interior.

Le studio a été conçu pour absorber le maximum de lumière naturelle et embellir les matériaux décorant la zone intérieure.

Das Atelier ist so angelegt, dass so viel Tageslicht wie möglich einfällt und das Material verschönert, mit dem der Raum geschmückt ist.

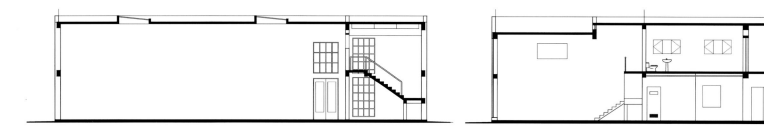

› Sections Sections Schnitte

Klinkowstein-Gillett Residence
Résidence Klinkowstein-Gillett
Haus Klinkowstein-Gillett

New York, USA

Robin Elmslie Osler designed this house for Tom Klinkowstein, a professor of journalism and the owner of the Media Arts consulting firm (specializing in the communications media) and Elisabeth Gillet, a furniture designer. Their respective interests required the architect to come up with answers to the contrasting sensibilities she discerned in them. The original space had little natural light, as it only entered on one side. Thus, the fusion of the two clients' sensibilities was achieved, in the architect's view, by incorporating materials that would facilitate the entrance of natural light. To achieve this, the space was subdivided using transparent glass panels and plastic-coated mesh screens. The transparent surfaces could become opaque in response to the intensity of the light and the movements of the house's occupants. The space was revitalized by the introduction of light and took on a new depth.

Robin Elmslie Osler a conçu cette maison pour un couple, Tom Klinkowstein, professeur de journalisme et propriétaire de l'agence Media Arts, spécialisée dans les médias et Elisabeth Gillett, dessinatrice d'accessoires. Etant donnée la nature de leurs intérêts respectifs, il était impératif de trouver une solution pour rapprocher leurs sensibilités contraires. La lumière ne pénétrant que d'un côté, l'espace ne recevait pas assez de lumière naturelle. Selon l'architecte, la fusion des deux sensibilités n'est possible qu'en intégrant des matériaux qui facilitent l'entrée de la lumière naturelle. Pour y parvenir, la division de l'espace se fait au moyen de vitres transparentes et de paravents en mailles plastifiées. Les surfaces transparentes deviennent opaques selon l'intensité de la lumière et du mouvement des occupants. L'espace, dynamisé par les variations de lumière, gagne en profondeur.

Robin Elmslie Osler entwarf dieses Haus für ein Paar, Tom Klinkowstein, Professor für Journalistik und Eigentümer der Beratungsgesellschaft Media Arts, die auf die Welt der Kommunikation spezialisiert ist, und Elisabeth Gillett, Accessoire-Designerin. Für dieses Paar musste eine Lösung gefunden werden, durch die sich ihre Interessen einander annähern. In den Räumen gibt es wenig Tageslicht, das nur von einer Seite einfällt. Die Verbindung der Empfindungswelten der Kunden wird, wie der Architekt unterstreicht, durch den Einsatz von Materialien erreicht, die das Tageslicht hereinlassen. Dazu wurde der Raum mit durchsichtigen Glaspaneelen und Wandschirmen aus plastifizierten Maschen unterteilt. Die transparenten Oberflächen werden je nach Lichtmenge und den Bewegungen der Bewohner undurchsichtig. Der Raum wird durch diese Lichtveränderungen belebt und gewinnt an Tiefe.

The scarcity of light in the interior determined the choice of highly reflective materials.

La faiblesse de l'éclairage intérieur a été déterminante dans le choix des matériaux dont la texture reflète la lumière.

Da die Räume recht dunkel waren, wählte der Architekt Materialien, deren Texturen Licht reflektieren.

› Plan Plan Grundriss

Veen Apartment
Appartement Veen
Appartement Veen

Amsterdam, Netherlands

Located in a residential area of picturesque brick houses dating from the 1930s, this apartment has a broad façade on the street. After examining a variety of layouts the different rooms, it was decided that they should be organized around a large central element, and that this nucleus should be used as the starting point for the creation of a new interior. So, the original doors were replaced with openings whose widths were proportional to the rooms they opened on to. Moldings and baseboards were done away with and the parquet floor was replaced with a polished cement finish that lends a degree of abstraction to the house-the rigor of its forms, on the other hand, is determined by the lighting. By strengthening the house's visual and spatial connections, the classical lines of this apartment have been transformed into a contemporary and dynamic residence.

Situé dans une zone résidentielle aux très pittoresques maisons en brique des années 30, cet appartement présente une large façade sur la rue. Après avoir étudié toutes les possibilités d'emplacement des espaces de vie, la balance a penché en faveur d'une organisation des pièces autour d'un grand distributeur central et de l'utilisation de ce noyau comme point de départ à la création d'un nouvel intérieur. Pour cela, les portes originales ont été substituées par des ouvertures d'une largeur proportionnelle aux chambres. Moulures et plinthes ont été supprimées et le parquet remplacé par un revêtement en ciment poli qui confère à l'habitation un certain degré d'abstraction. La rigueur des formes, quant à elle, est sublimée par l'éclairage. En mettant l'accent sur les liens visuels et spatiaux, cet appartement aux lignes classiques s'est métamorphosé en une résidence contemporaine emprunte de dynamisme.

Dieses Appartement, das in einem Wohngebiet mit malerischen Ziegelhäusern aus den Dreißigerjahren liegt, hat eine breite Fassade zur Straße hin. Nachdem verschiedene Möglichkeiten der Raumaufteilung überdacht wurden, entschloss man sich, die Räume um einen großen, zentral gelegenen Verteiler herum zu organisieren und diesen Kern als Ausgangspunkt für die neue Raumgestaltung zu nehmen. Dazu wurden die ursprünglichen Türen durch breite Öffnungen zu den Räumen ersetzt. Leisten und Sockel wurden entfernt und das Parkett wurde durch einen Boden aus poliertem Zement ersetzt, der die Wohnung etwas abstrakt wirken lässt. Die formale Strenge wird durch die Beleuchtung unterstrichen. Durch die Verstärkung der visuellen und räumlichen Verbindungen wurde aus dieser klassischen Wohnung eine zeitgemäße und dynamische Wohnumgebung.

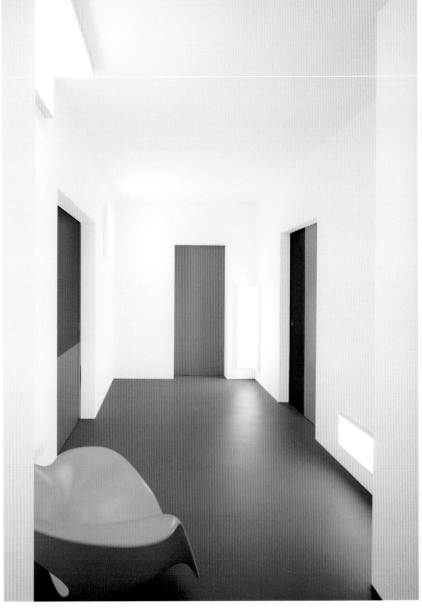

The doors, frames and original moldings were eliminated to strengthen the space and to increase the amount of light in the interior.

Les portes, plinthes et moulures d'origine ont été éliminées pour accentuer la notion d'espace et accroître la luminosité à l'intérieur de l'habitation.

Die originalen Türen, Rahmen und Leisten wurden entfernt, um den Raum zu unterstreichen und heller zu machen.

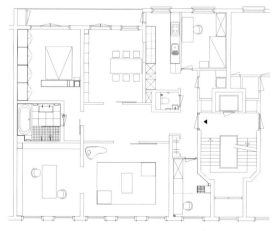

› **Plan** Plan Grundriss

Vos Residence
Résidence Vos
Haus Vos

Amsterdam, Netherlands

This house is a perfect example of composition-al rationalism: fitted between two buildings, it rises uninterrupted between the vertical planes of its structure and the horizontal planes of its windows. It is able thus to create a visual tension that generates a highly dynamic composition, seemingly springing from the earth in the form of a transparent box. The main façade opens on to the street and is only interrupted by the entrance to the garage, which can barely be seen when it is closed. The house is distributed over four different levels: the basement contains a storeroom, bathroom and study; the main level has the entrance to the house, in addition to the garage, a bedroom and another bathroom; the first floor holds the kitchen and dining room; and finally, on the second floor, there is a spacious living room filled with natural light filtered through skylights in the ceiling.

Cette maison est l'exemple parfait d'une composition rationaliste. Encastrée entre deux constructions, elle s'élève dans un jeu continu entre les plans verticaux de la structure et les plans horizontaux des fenêtres pour créer une tension visuelle génératrice de dynamisme au niveau de la composition. Elle semble surgir du terrain comme une boîte tout en transparence. La façade principale atteint la rue et n'est interrompue que par l'entrée au garage, à peine visible une fois fermée. L'habitation s'articule sur quatre niveaux : le sous-sol héberge une réserve, une salle de bains et un studio, le rez-de-chaussée comprend l'entrée, le garage, une chambre et une autre salle de bains, le premier étage accueille la cuisine et la salle à manger ; et enfin, le deuxième étage, un vaste salon baigné de lumière naturelle grâce aux velux du toit.

Dieses Wohnhaus ist ein perfektes Beispiel für den gestalterischen Rationalismus. Es steht zwischen zwei Gebäuden und erhebt sich in einem durchgehenden Spiel zwischen den vertikalen Ebenen der Struktur und den horizontalen Ebenen der Fenster, so dass eine visuelle Spannung entsteht, die die Gestaltung sehr dynamisch wirken und das Gebäude wie einen transparente Kasten dem Grundstück entspringen lässt. Die Hauptfassade reicht bis zur Straße und wird nur durch den Garageneingang unterbrochen, der kaum bemerkbar ist, wenn er geschlossen bleibt. Das Haus besteht aus vier Ebenen, im Keller befinden sich ein Lagerraum, ein Bad und ein Atelier, im Erdgeschoss der Eingang, die Garage, ein Schlafzimmer und ein weiteres Bad. Im ersten Stock liegt die Küche und das Speisezimmer, und im zweiten Stock ein großes Wohnzimmer, in das durch Dachfenster reichlich Tageslicht fällt.

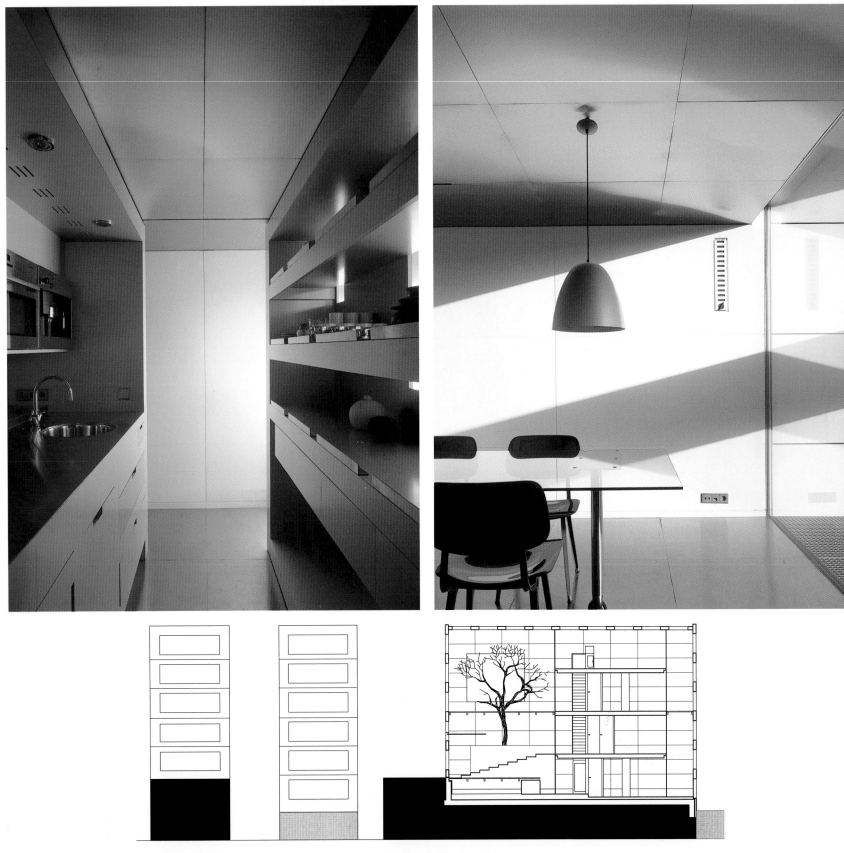

› Elevations Élévations Aufrisse

› Section Section Schnitt

FOB A-001 Houses
Maisons FOB A-001
Häuser FOB A-001

Osaka, Japan

The architects of this house started with the idea of creating a group of small apartments as an alternative to the mass production of houses. The interior of the FOB A-001 houses is based on the principle of visual continuity; accordingly, an open space was designed, with detail kept to the minimum. A metal staircase leads to the highest part of the house, where a series of bedrooms are laid out in an L-shape, giving rise to an outer ring of rooms that are visible from any point in the interior garden. However, the essence of the project lies in the central void: in its center lies the garden, while the house rises around it as though to protect this central space from the exterior. The elements are distributed in keeping with the premises of a functional, hermetic and cubic architecture of sparse details.

Les architectes sont partis de l'idée de créer un ensemble d'appartements, en alternative à la production massive de logements. L'intérieur des maisons FOB A-001 est basé sur le principe de la continuité visuelle qui crée un espace ouvert dominé par l'économie de détails. Un escalier métallique conduit à la partie la plus élevée de l'habitation, où une enfilade de chambres en forme de L s'articule le long de l'intérieur de l'unité créant une ceinture d'espaces visibles de n'importe quel endroit du jardin intérieur. Toutefois, l'essence du projet est le vide central : en son centre, il intègre le jardin, et sur le pourtour, l'habitation s'élève comme pour protéger l'espace central de l'extérieur. Les éléments s'articulent selon les critères d'une architecture fonctionnelle, sobre en détails, hermétique et cubique.

Die Architekten wollten eine Gruppe von Wohnungen schaffen, die eine Alternative zur Massenproduktion darstellen. Die Räume der Häuser FOB A-001 basieren auf dem Prinzip der visuellen Kontinuität, auf Grundlage dessen ein offener Raum mit wenig Details geschaffen wurde. Eine Metalltreppe führt zum oberen Teil der Wohnung, wo sich eine Reihe von Zimmern in L-Form verteilen, so dass ein Gürtel von Räumen entsteht, die von dem gesamten Garten im Inneren aus sichtbar sind. Das wichtigste Element der Wohneinheiten ist jedoch der Innenhof, in dem sich ein Garten befindet. Um den Garten verteilt sich die Wohnung, so als ob sie ihn vor der Außenwelt schützen wolle. Die Elemente werden nach den Grundsätzen einer funktionellen Architektur verteilt, einfache Details, hermetisch und kubisch.

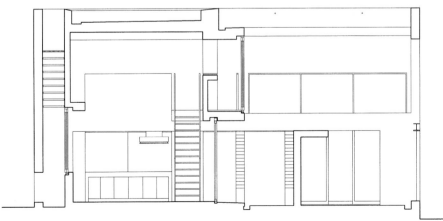

› Section Section Schnitt

2/5 House
Maison 2/5
Haus 2/5

Nishinomiya, Japan

The 2/5 house forms part of a series of experimental buildings that are based on an exploration of space and how it interacts with its surroundings. The total surface area is divided into five identical strips, in which interior spaces merge with gardens and terraces. The house is delimited, to the east and to the west, by double-height concrete walls, while the northern façade is granted privacy by a dense PVC mesh. The façades that open on to the street are enclosed within a folded aluminum screen, which has been perforated to provide views of the ramp leading to the garage. An independent door leads to a hallway that stretches along one the side of the house and connects the succession of courtyards and habitable rooms. Although this house echoes certain elements of traditional Japanese architecture, it responds in thoroughly imaginative ways to the requirements of contemporary life.

La maison 2/5 fait partie d'une série de constructions expérimentales basées sur l'exploration de l'espace et de ses relations avec l'environnement. La superficie totale est divisée en cinq franges égales intercalées d'espaces intérieurs dotés de jardins et de terrasses. L'habitation est limitée, à l'est et à l'ouest, par des murs de béton sur deux hauteurs : sur la face nord, un treillis épais en PVC préserve son intimité. La façade donnant sur la rue est protégée par un écran d'aluminium renforcé et perforé qui laisse percevoir la rampe menant au garage. Une porte indépendante s'ouvre sur un passage qui parcourt longitudinalement un des côtés de la maison reliant ainsi l'enfilade de patios et les zones habitables. Même si la construction reflète l'architecture japonaise traditionnelle, la maison met en scène l'imaginaire pour satisfaire les impératifs de la vie contemporaine.

Das Haus 2/5 gehört zu einer Reihe von experimentellen Bauten, die auf der Erforschung des Raums und der Wechselbeziehung zur Umgebung beruhen. Die Gesamtfläche unterteilt sich in fünf gleiche Streifen, auf denen sich Innenräume mit Gärten und Terrassen abwechseln. Das Haus wird im Osten und im Westen von Betonmauern doppelter Höhe begrenzt, und im Norden von einem dichten PVC-Netz von der Außenwelt abgetrennt. Die Fassade zur Straße hin wird durch einen gefalteten und perforierten Aluminiumschirm geschlossen, der die Rampe durchschimmern lässt, die zur Garage führt. Eine unabhängige Tür führt zum Gang, der längs an den Seiten des Hauses vorbeiführt und die aufeinander folgenden Höfe und Wohnräume miteinander verbindet. Obwohl das Gebäude von der traditionellen, japanischen Architektur beeinflusst ist, wurde es mit viel Einfallsreichtum an die Anforderungen des modernen Lebens angepasst.

Designed for an intrepid pair of clients, this prototype aims to be a solution in tune with every aspect of domestic life.

Conçu pour des clients audacieux, ce prototype prétend être la solution parfaite pour résoudre tous les aspects de la vie familiale.

Dieser, für sehr offene Kunden angelegte Prototyp, soll eine geeignete Lösung für alle Aspekte des häuslichen Lebens darstellen.

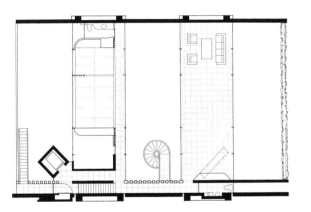

› First floor Premier étage Erstes Obergeschoss

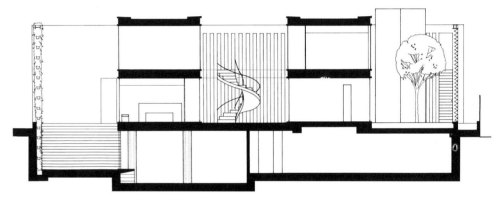

› Section Section Schnitt

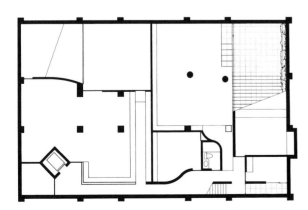

› Basement Sous-sol Kellergeschoss

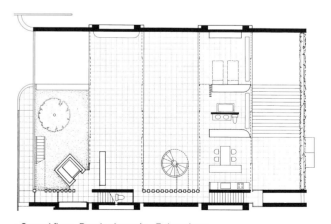

› Ground floor Rez-de-chaussée Erdgeschoss

The house presents an altered version of the traditional courtyard – the surface has been fragmented to alternate interior spaces with terraces.

L'habitation propose une interprétation du patio traditionnel : la surface est fragmentée pour intercaler des espaces intérieurs dotés de terrasses.

Das Haus verfügt über eine veränderte Version des traditionellen Innenhofes, die Fläche ist unterteilt, so dass sich Innenräume mit Terrassen abwechseln.

The desire to integrate exterior spaces into the interior was achieved through sliding glass doors, which open to unify the different spaces.

L'intégration des surfaces extérieures aux intérieures s'obtient grâce à des portes coulissantes de verre qui s'effacent pour unifier l'espace.

Die Außenbereiche werden mithilfe von Schiebetüren aus Glas in die Räume integriert. Diese können verschoben werden, um die Räume zu verbinden.

Residence in Antwerpen
Résidence à Anvers
Wohnung in Antwerpen

Antwerpen, Belgium

The design of this apartment aimed to maintain the structure of two existing areas and to convey a sensation of freedom. Each part is delimited by an ample central corridor, whose sliding walls can be moved easily. On one side, a toilet and open shower transform the entrance hall into a large, white bathroom. At the other end, the oak finishes of the bedroom and the grey of the walls provide a greater degree of intimacy. The boundary between the daytime and the nighttime areas is enlarged by a glass wall. The ample living room – divided by a large column – contains a dining room table and an armchair that sits right across from the kitchen, while the area for reading and relaxing is located to the right, comfortably furnished with rugs and blankets.

La conception de cet appartement a voulu conserver la structure de deux zones existantes et transmettre une sensation de liberté. Chaque partie est délimitée par un vaste couloir central, dont les murs coulissants peuvent être facilement déplacés. Sur un côté, un lavabo et une zone de douche ouverte métamorphosent cette partie du vestibule en une grande salle de bains blanche. A l'autre extrémité, les finitions en chêne de la chambre à coucher et les murs gris créent plus d'intimité. La limite entre la zone de jour et de nuit disparaît grâce à un mur de verre. Le vaste salon, divisé par une colonne, accueille une table de salle à manger et un fauteuil qui se trouve juste en face de la cuisine. La zone de lecture et de repos se trouve sur la droite, bénéficiant du confort des tapis et des plaids.

Bei der Gestaltung dieser Wohnung sollte die Struktur der bereits existierenden Bereiche beibehalten werden und das Gefühl von Freiheit entstehen. Jeder Teil wurde von einem weiten, zentralen Korridor begrenzt, dessen gleitenden Wände leicht verschoben werden können. Auf einer Seite bilden eine Toilette und ein offener Duschbereich einen Teil am Eingang eines langen, weißen Bades. Auf der anderen Seite entstand durch die Eichenverkleidung des Schlafzimmers und die grauen Wände eine intimere Atmosphäre. Die Begrenzung zwischen den Bereichen für den Tag und die Nacht wird durch eine Glaswand erweitert. Das große, von einer Säule geteilte Wohnzimmer enthält einen Esstisch und einen Lehnstuhl, der genau der Küche gegenüber steht. Auf der rechten Seite befindet sich ein Leseraum zum Entspannen, hier liegen Teppiche und Decken.

The glass doors are framed by black panels that interact with the black frames hanging in the entrance hall.

Les portes en verre sont encadrées de panneaux noirs qui rappellent les cadres de même couleur suspendus dans le couloir.

Die Glastüren werden von schwarzen Paneelen umschlossen, die eine Verbindung zu den schwarzen Rahmen herstellen, die im Eingangsbereich hängen.

The bathroom area is located beside one of the corridors and can be integrated or separated by opening the large sliding doors.

La zone de la salle de bains se trouve à côté d'un couloir. De grandes portes coulissantes permettent de l'intégrer ou de la séparer.

Das Badezimmer befindet sich neben dem Eingangsbereich und es kann durch große Schiebetüren geöffnet oder abgetrennt werden.

The sliding doors can be closed to obtain a better layout of the living spaces.

Les portes coulissantes du couloir peuvent être fermées pour parvenir à une meilleure distribution des espaces de vie.

Die Schiebetüren im Eingangsbereich können geschlossen werden, um die Räume besser aufzuteilen.

Dwelling in Tel Aviv
Habitation à Tel Aviv
Wohnung in Tel Aviv

Tel Aviv, Israel

This house is a reflection on the art of contemporary living. The program foresaw the creation of a living room that could be transformed into a bedroom, to do this, a space was designed to guarantee the occupants' privacy and the isolation needed to fulfil both funcions. The two areas meet at a sliding door that allows for a constant connection between the two; when the situation requires it, however, is it possible for the two areas to be isolated from one another by simply sliding the door closed. The details of the construction and the decorative elements lend a personal air to the project; the lighting, which takes advantage of the natural light entering through the large windows, is complemented by lamps in the darker corners.

Cette habitation est le reflet d'une réflexion sur l'habitat contemporain. Le projet a programmé la création d'un salon qui puisse se transformer en chambre à coucher. La conception de l'espace permet donc d'assurer l'intimité et l'isolement nécessaires pour pouvoir satisfaire aux deux fonctions. Les deux univers se rencontrent par le biais d'une porte coulissante qui leur permet de communiquer constamment l'un avec l'autre, si nécessaire. Cependant, il est possible de convertir ces deux sphères en espaces privés en faisant tout simplement glisser la porte. Les détails de construction et les éléments décoratifs donnent du caractère au projet. L'éclairage qui bénéficie de la lumière naturelle venant des grandes baies vitrées, est complété par des points de lumière additionnels dans les zones plus retirées.

Diese Wohnung ist eine Art Nachdenken über das zeitgenössische Wohnen. Es sollte ein Wohnzimmer geschaffen werden, das man in ein Schlafzimmer verwandeln kann. So entstand ein Raum, der genügend Privatsphäre besitzt, damit er beiden Zwecken dienen kann. Die beiden Bereiche treffen an einer Schiebetür aufeinander, die eine ständige Kommunikation ermöglicht, falls es die Situation erfordert, die aber auch beide Bereiche durch einfaches Schieben der Tür voneinander abtrennen kann. Die konstruktiven Einzelheiten und die dekorativen Elemente verleihen diesem Gebäude seine Persönlichkeit. Tageslicht strömt durch die großen Fenster ein, und in den weiter von den Fenstern entfernten Bereichen wurden zusätzlich künstliche Lichtquellen installiert.

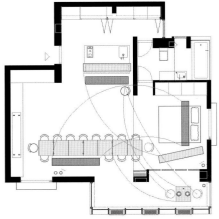

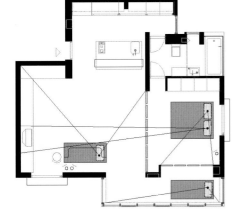

› Plans Plans Grundrisse

Residence in New York
Résidence new-yorkaise
Wohnung in New York

New York, USA

The owner of this magnificent home with views of Central Park is an art collector who needed sufficient space to be able to display his collection. The daytime area exudes the spirit of an art gallery: the terrazzo floors in the foyer and the dining room are immaculate, even cold. The meticulously designed double ceiling, which hides the lighting system, includes a series of lamps focused on the original artworks from the owner's collection. The main bedroom is dominated by a print by the photographer Uta Barth. The serenity emanating from the bedroom continues in the bathroom, where limestone floor and plaster walls contrast with marble tiles and Corian countertops. The furnishings combine pieces by prestigious designers, such as the dining-room table by Jean Nouvel and the lamp by Alison Berger.

Le propriétaire de cette magnifique maison avec vues sur Central Park, est un collectionneur d'art en quête d'un vaste espace pour pouvoir exposer sa collection. La zone de jour est imprégnée de l'esprit d'une galerie d'art. Les sols sont immaculés, presque froids, en terrasse à l'entrée et dans la salle à manger. Le double toit, parfaitement conçu, masque l'éclairage doté d'une série de lampes orientées pour mettre en valeur l'originalité et la beauté des œuvres d'art. Dans la chambre principale, le regard est attiré par certaines œuvres photographiques signées Uta Barth. La sérénité qui émane de la chambre à coucher se poursuit dans la salle de bains où la pierre calcaire du carrelage et la chaux des murs contrastent avec la mosaïque de marbre et les parements en Corian. Les éléments de mobilier affichent des designs de créateurs prestigieux, à l'instar de la salle à manger de Jean Nouvel ou de la lampe d'Alison Berger.

Der Eigentümer dieser wundervollen Wohnung mit Blick auf den Central Park ist ein Kunstsammler, der viel Platz brauchte, um seine Kollektion auszustellen. Der Bereich für den Tag ist vom Geist einer Kunstgalerie geprögt, die Böden wirken rein, fast kalt. Die Böden im Eingangsbereich und Speisezimmer sind mit Terrazzo belegt. Die doppelte Decke, mit großer Sorgfalt entworfen, verbirgt die Beleuchtung, zu der eine Reihe von Scheinwerfern gehören, die die Einzigartigkeit und Schönheit der Kunstwerke unterstreichen. Im Hauptschlafzimmer hängen Fotografien der Fotografin Uta Barth. Die Klarheit, die vom Schlafzimmer ausstrahlt wird, setzt sich im Bad fort. Hier bilden der Kalkstein des Bodens und der Gips der Wände einen Kontrast zu dem Marmormosaik und den Badezimmeraufsätzen von Corian. Die Möbel stammen von berühmten Designern, der Esstisch zum Beispiel von Jean Nouvel und die Lampe von Alison Berger.

Various specialists offered different ideas for the lighting design, intended to show off the pieces in the collection in their full glory.

Différents spécialistes collaborent aux diverses propositions de conception de l'éclairage pour exalter la beauté des œuvres exposées.

Verschiedene Fachleute haben an den unterschiedlichen Entwürfen der Beleuchtung mitgearbeitet, um die Schönheit der ausgestellten Werke zu unterstreichen.

The overall sensation is of neatness, with attention inexorably drawn to the works of art, the true protagonists of the space.

L'ensemble transmet une impression de perfection et le regard est attiré par les œuvres d'art, les vraies protagonistes de l'espace.

Das Interieur strahlt ein Gefühl von Reinheit aus und der Blick wird auf die Kunstwerke gelenkt, die wahren Protagonisten der Räume.

To underline the fluidity between spaces and the connections between the various areas, the bathroom is separated from the rest of the house by a curtain.

La salle de bains est séparée du reste de la chambre par le biais d'un rideau pour souligner la fluidité de l'espace et la communication entre les différents univers.

Das Bad wird durch eine Gardine vom Rest der Wohnung abgetrennt, um das Fließen des Raumes und die Verbindung zwischen den verschiedenen Bereichen zu unterstreichen.

House in Honda
Maison à Honda
Haus in Honda

Honda, Colombia

This house was built on two lots that were originally occupied by residences and warehouses, of which only the façades and a smattering of colonial-style stone walls remained. The new project was conceived as a sequence of bright spaces – built around the remains of the old buildings – which, even though they may at first seem utterly chaotic, are arranged along carefully calculated visual axes. The spaces in the house open on to an unusual series of outdoor spaces: a courtyard planted with aromatic herbs, a garden with citrus trees and a gravel patio. The lighting, designed by Guillermo Arias, is a determining factor that highlights the character of the original walls, the textures and the vegetation.

Cette habitation a été construite sur deux parcelles, occupées auparavant par des logements et des entrepôts dont il ne restait que les façades et quelques murs de pierre de style colonial. Le nouveau projet propose une série d'espaces diaphanes -développés à partir des ruines des anciens édifices- dont la disposition, malgré une certaine impression première de désordre, est conçue le long d'axes visuels bien étudiés. Les espaces s'ouvrent sur des extérieurs aux caractéristiques particulières : un patio d'herbes aromatiques, un jardin d'agrumes ou un patio de galets. L'éclairage conçu par Guillermo Arias est un élément déterminant qui exalte le caractère des murs d'origine, des textures et de la végétation.

Dieses Haus wurde auf zwei Parzellen errichtet, auf denen einst zwei Häuser und Lager standen, von denen nur die Fassaden und einige Steinmauern im kolonialen Stil erhalten waren. Das neue Bauvorhaben sah eine Sequenz von transparenten Räumen vor, die auf den Ruinen der alten Gebäude errichtet werden sollten. Auf den ersten Blick wirkt das Konzept ungeordnet, aber die Räume wurden entlang gut durchdachter, visueller Achsen angelegt. Die Wohnumgebungen öffnen sich zu einer vielfältigen Außenwelt mit besonderen Kennzeichen, ein Hof voller aromatischer Kräuter, ein Garten mit Zitrusfrüchten und ein Hof mit Kieselsteinen. Die von Guillermo Arias entworfene Beleuchtung ist ein entscheidendes Gestaltungselement und unterstreicht den Charakter der Originalmauern, die Textur und die Vegetation.

Each space in the house opens on to a different and unique outdoor space.

Chaque espace de l'habitation s'ouvre sur un extérieur différent et unique.

Jede Wohnumgebung des Hauses öffnet sich zu einer anderen, einzigartigen Außenwelt.

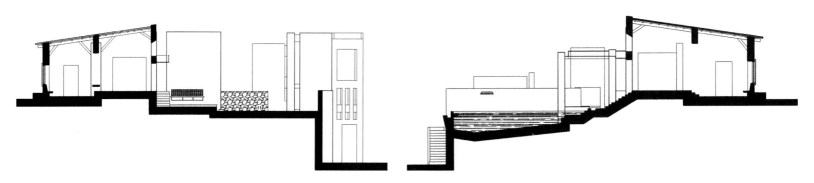

› Sections Sections Schnitte

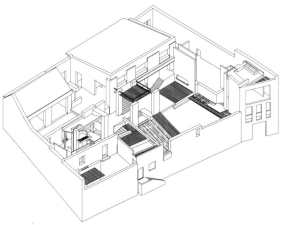

› Perspective Perspective Perspektivzeichnung

House without walls
Maison sans murs
Haus ohne Wände

Tokyo, Japan

Tezuka Architects is today one of Japan's most emblematic architectural firms. Projects such as the House without Walls is one of its most representative projects. It is situated on an expansive lot that offered a unique opportunity to open the house to the surrounding landscape, in a manner reminiscent of a rural shelter or house. As the building only occupies 20% of the site, an open area was maintained around it to create a truly uninterrupted space; the result is a genuinely open house. Thanks to its lightweight steel structure, the load is distributed towards a central nucleus and along two slender columns; this enabled the architect to eliminate the perimeter walls and to create a totally open house. The three floors of the building seem to float in the air, surrounded by trees, and they give off an air of freshness and intimacy.

Le cabinet Tezuka Architects, est en réalité un des bureaux d'architecture phare du Japon. Parmi ses œuvres les plus représentatives, citons les projets comme celui de la Maison sans murs, située sur un grand terrain qui offre la possibilité unique d'ouvrir l'habitation sur le paysage environnant. Ce projet n'est pas sans rappeler une maison-refuge à la campagne. L'habitation n'occupant que 20% du terrain est entourée de toute une zone ouverte qui crée un espace continu, une véritable maison ouverte. Grâce à une structure en acier léger, les charges sont réparties sur un noyau central et sur deux colonnes étroites. Cela a permis d'éliminer les murs du pourtour et d'ouvrir entièrement la maison. Les trois étages de l'édifice semblent flotter dans l'air et sont entourés d'arbres que transmettent une sensation de fraîcheur et d'intimité.

Tezuka Architects ist zur Zeit eines der berühmtesten Architekturstudios Japans. Zu den erfolgreichsten Projekten dieses Studios gehört das Haus ohne Wände, das auf einem großen Gelände steht, das die einzigartige Möglichkeit bot, das Haus zur umgebenden Landschaft hin zu öffnen. So wirkt das Gebäude wie eine Hütte auf dem Lande. Das Gebäude nimmt nur 20% des Grundstücks ein, so dass man um das Haus herum Platz frei lassen konnte, wodurch ein ununterbrochen Raum entstand, ein wirklich offenes Haus. Über eine leichte Stahlstruktur werden die Lasten über einen zentralen Kern und zwei schmale Säulen verteilt. So konnte man die umgebenden Mauern eliminieren und das Haus vollständig öffnen. Die drei Stockwerke des Gebäudes scheinen in der Luft zu schweben und sind von Bäumen umgeben, die die Räume frisch und geschützt wirken lassen.

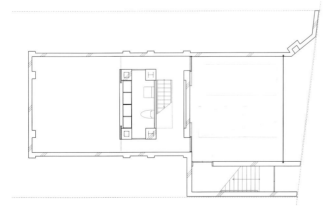

› Ground floor Rez-de-chaussée Erdgeschoss

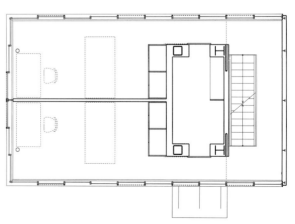

› First floor Premier étage Erstes Obergeschoss

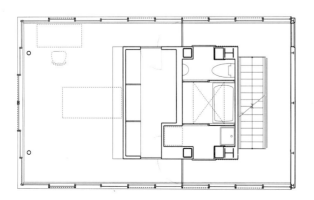

› Second floor Deuxième étage Zweites Obergeschoss

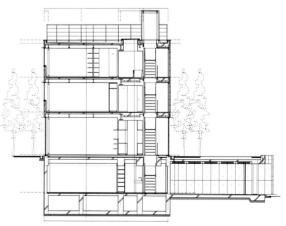

› Section Section Schnitt

M House
Maison M
Haus M

Tokyo, Japan

This south-facing house, located in a residential district in the center of Tokyo, occupies a 23,250 sq. ft. site. The architects decided to open the house to the exterior without sacrificing the privacy of the rooms inside. The clients required two studios, a guest bedroom, two bathrooms, a parking space, a bedroom for the children they were planning to have, and a spacious living room. Some of these rooms, such as the main bedroom, the guest bedroom and garage, needed to be somewhat more independent from the other rooms in the house – for precisely this reason there were located on the top floor. The dining room, studio and other open spaces were located on the lower level; here, the noise from the busy street is impossible to discern, making this part of the house is a perfect area in which to relax.

Cette maison, située dans un quartier résidentiel du centre de Tokyo, occupe un terrain de 2.160 m². La façade est orientée vers le sud. Les architectes ont décidé d'ouvrir l'habitation vers l'extérieur sans nuire à l'intimité des espaces intérieurs. Les clients voulaient deux bureaux, une chambre d'amis, deux salles de bains, une place de parking, une chambre pour leurs futurs enfants et un salon spacieux. Certains de ces espaces de vie, à l'instar de la chambre principale, de la chambre d'amis et du garage devant être indépendants du reste de l'espace, ont été installés sur le niveau principal. La salle à manger, le bureau et d'autres espaces ouverts ont été placés au rez-de-chaussée : loin du bruit de la rue voisine, cette zone de la maison se métamorphose en lieu de détente idéal.

Dieses Haus in einem Wohnbezirk im Zentrum von Tokio steht auf einem 2 160 m² großen Grundstück. Die Fassade liegt in Richtung Süden. Die Architekten entschieden sich dafür, das Haus nach außen zu öffnen, ohne dass dabei die Privatsphäre der Räume verloren geht. Die Kunden benötigten zwei Ateliers, ein Gästezimmer, zwei Badezimmer, einen Parkplatz, ein Schlafzimmer für den künftigen Nachwuchs und ein großes Wohnzimmer. Einige dieser Räume wie das Schlafzimmer des Paares, das Gästezimmer und die Garage mussten unabhängig vom Rest der Räumlichkeiten sein. Deshalb liegen sie im ersten Stock. Das Speisezimmer, das Atelier und die anderen, offenen Räume liegen im Erdgeschoss. Hier hört man den Lärm der nahe gelegenen Straße nicht, so dass dieser Bereich zum idealen Ort der Entspannung wird.

The façade that opens on to the street is designed as a succession of straight planes with discreet openings that connect with the exterior.

La façade qui donne sur la rue est formée d'une succession de plans rectilignes dotés d'ouvertures discrètes qui communiquent avec l'extérieur.

Die Fassade zur Straße ist wie eine Aufeinanderfolge von geraden Ebenen angelegt, die diskret die Öffnungen zeigen, die mit der Außenwelt verbinden.

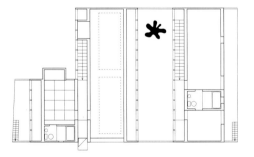

› First floor Premier étage Erstes Obergeschoss

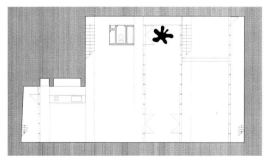

› Ground floor Rez-de-chaussée Erdgeschoss

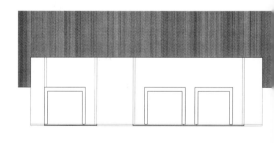

› Section Section Schnitt

The communal areas, such as the living room, are located on the lower level to insulate them from the noise coming from the street.

Les espaces communs, comme la salle à manger, se trouvent au niveau inférieur afin de les isoler du bruit de la circulation.

Die gemeinsamen Räume wie das Wohnzimmer befinden sich auf der unteren Ebene, in die kein Lärm dringt.

House-Mirador
Maison mirador
Haus und Aussichtsterrasse

Olot, Spain

This house, designed by Aranda, Pigem and Vilalta, is a good example of simplicity, as it avoids superficial elements that could confuse the onlooker's perception of its spaces, qualities and specificity. Situated at the bottom of a gentle slope, the building appears as a floating lookout tower overlooking the countryside around Girona. Following the guidelines for the construction of a pavilion, the metal structure and the roof define the glass enclosures of the house. The entrance to the house is situated in the void created between the two volumes that make up the house, one of which contains the service areas, while the other contains the bedrooms and living room. This project, a combination of impeccable stone surfaces and transparent façades, is distinguished by an interplay of light and views from the interior.

Cette maison d'Aranda, Pigem et Vilalta est l'exemple même de la simplicité, évitant les éléments superflus capables d'entraver la perception des espaces, leur qualité et leur spécificité. Situé à l'extrémité d'une pente douce, l'édifice ressemble à un mirador flottant tourné vers la campagne de Gérone. Suivant les critères de construction d'un pavillon, les fondations et la couverture définissent les parois en verre de la maison. L'accès à la maison est formé par l'enfoncement entre les deux volumes qui la constituent. L'un abrite les zones de service et l'autre accueille les chambres et les salons. Ce projet, alliant à merveille les surfaces de pierre parfaites et les façades transparentes, attire le regard par ses jeux de lumière et les vues qu'il offre depuis l'intérieur.

Dieses Haus von Aranda, Pigem und Vilalta ist ein gutes Beispiel für Schlichtheit. Oberflächliche Elemente, die die Wahrnehmung der Räume, ihrer Schönheit und Besonderheit trüben könnten, wurden vermieden. Es liegt oben auf einer leichten Anhöhe und wirkt wie eine schwebende Aussichtsterrasse, von der man auf die Felder der Region Girona blickt. In dem wie ein Pavillon angelegten Haus begrenzen Deckplatte und Dach die verglasten Wände des Gebäudes. Der Eingangsbereich liegt in der Öffnung zwischen den beiden Gebäudeteilen, aus denen das Haus besteht. In einem Teil befinden sich die funktionellen Räume und in dem anderen die Schlafzimmer und die Wohnzimmer. Dieses Gebäude mit seinen makellos Oberflächen aus Stein und transparenten Fassaden fällt durch das Spiel mit dem Licht und dem Ausblick auf, den man aus den Räumen hat.

A glass plinth emphasizes the feeling of lightness and allows light into the basement.

Un socle de verre exalte la sensation de légèreté et illumine le sous-sol.

Ein Glassockel unterstreicht den Eindruck von Leichtigkeit und lässt Tageslicht in den Keller dringen.

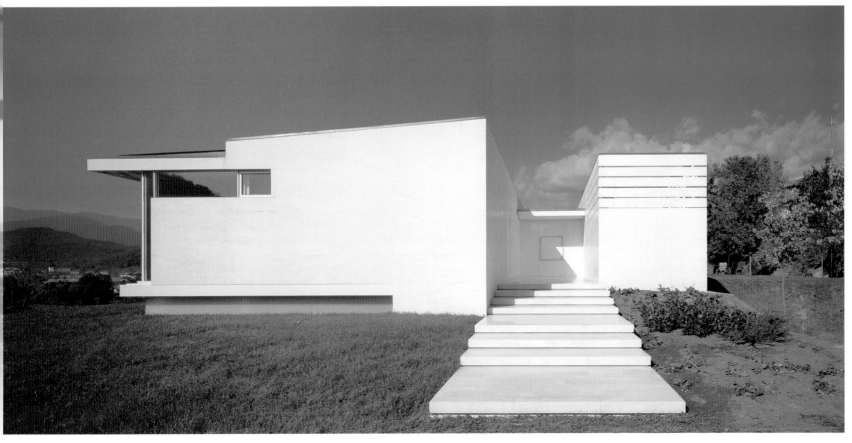

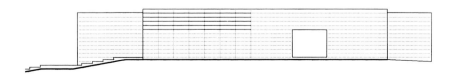
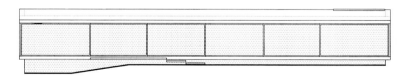

› Elevations Élévations Aufrisse

Subtlety and simplicity are the keys to this project, which distinguishes itself in the details of its construction.

Elégance et simplicité constituent l'essence de ce projet qui frappe par la perfection des détails de construction.

Subtilität und Einfachheit sind die Schlüsselelemente dieses Gebäudes, dass durch die Perfektion der konstruktiven Einzelheiten auffällt.

Dwelling in Izu
Habitation à Izu
Haus in Izu

Izu, Japan

With this house, the architect Shigeru Ban aimed to create an open and free space that would be defined by an absolute rationality of structure and construction. The exterior of the house is clad in galvanized steel and aluminum-and-glass panels, while the interior walls were clad in plaster tiles. Located at the top of a gentle hill that rolls down to the shore, the house enjoys unparalleled views of the sea. When Ban arrived at the site for the first time, his first reaction was to mentally frame the striking panorama that unfolded before his eyes. The idea thus came to him to transform the structure of the house into a frame of enormous dimensions: a 65-ft-long by 8-ft-tall opening would cross the house from one end to the other to frame the continuously changing panorama, and provide a prime spot from which the house's lucky occupants could enjoy this view.

En concevant cette maison, l'architecte Shigeru Ban a voulu créer un espace ouvert et dégagé, défini par une rationalité structurelle et constructive absolue. L'extérieur de l'habitation est constitué d'acier galvanisé, de panneaux d'aluminium et de verre, tandis que l'intérieur est recouvert de plaques de plâtre. Situé sur les hauteurs d'une colline en pente douce qui descend jusqu'au bord de la mer, l'édifice jouit de vues imprenables sur l'océan. Lorsque Ban arriva pour la première fois sur le terrain de la future maison, sa première réaction fut de visionner, à l'instar d'un tableau, le splendide panorama qui se déroulait devant ses yeux. C'est ainsi qu'est née l'idée de transformer la structure de l'édifice en un immense cadre : une ouverture de 20 m de large sur 2,5 m de haut, traversant l'édifice de part en part, encadre le paysage qui change constamment, au grand bonheur des habitants privilégiés de la maison.

Der Architekt Shigeru Ban schuf mit diesem Haus einen offenen und freien Raum, der durch die absolute strukturelle und konstruktive Rationalität geprägt ist. Das Haus ist von außen mit galvanisiertem Stahl und Paneelen aus Aluminium und Glas verkleidet, im Inneren mit Gipsplatten. Es steht oben auf einem sanften Hügel, der am Ufer des Meeres endet. Man hat einen wundervollen Blick auf den Ozean. Als Ban zum ersten Mal das Grundstück betrat, auf dem er das Haus errichten sollte, hat er im Geiste zunächst den wundervollen Ausblick umrahmt, den er vor sich hatte. So entstand die Idee, die Struktur des Gebäudes in einen riesigen Rahmen zu verwandeln, eine 20 m lange und 2,5 m hohe Öffnung, die das Gebäude von einer Seite zur anderen durchkreuzt und das wechselhafte Bild der Landschaft umrahmt. Die privilegierten Bewohner dieses Hauses können in diesen Anblick eintauchen.

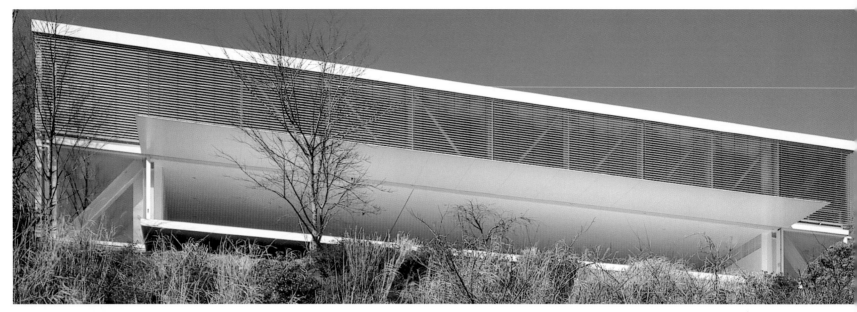

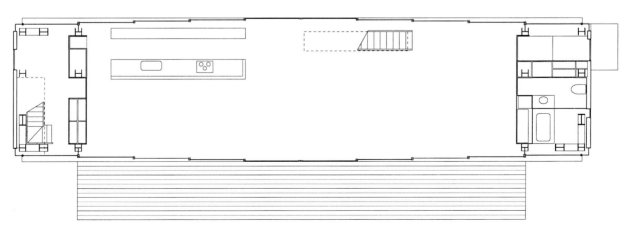

› Ground floor Rez-de-chaussée Erdgeschoss

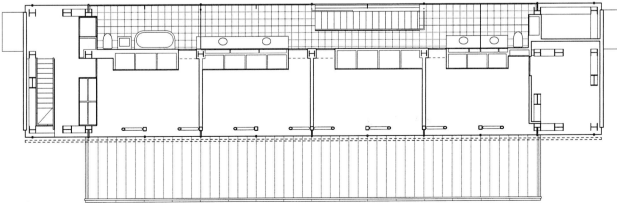

› First floor Premier étage Erstes Obergeschoss

Gamma-Issa House
Habitation Gamma-Issa
Haus Gamma-Issa

São Paulo, Brazil

This house is located in the neighborhood of Alto de Pinheiros, in São Paulo, a city that – in the words of the architect himself – is perhaps the least beautiful of all the cities in the world. A great white envelope encloses the perimeter and insulates the building from the surrounding context so as to create an eyecatching personal landscape. From the very beginning, the clients had proposed a very specific program: a shelf of gigantic proportions would occupy the entirety of the double-height living room, which would be complemented by double-height windows that would open on to the garden. Furthermore, the house was to have a pool, a kitchen with an orange dining room table, two marble staircases bathed in natural light and a tailor-made studio. Overall, the clients sought sophisticated spaces of elegant proportions that would establish a constant dialogue with the exterior.

Cette maison est située dans la zone de Alto de Pinheiros à São Paulo, une ville qui, selon les propres paroles de l'architecte, est peut-être la moins belle du monde. Un grand revêtement blanc fait fonction de mur d'enceinte et isole l'édifice du contexte ambiant pour créer un paysage particulier qui attire le regard. Les clients ont développé le projet à partir d'un principe de base : un système d'étagères aux grandes dimensions entièrement dédié au salon à double hauteur, doté d'immenses baies vitrées donnant sur le jardin, avec une piscine, une cuisine avec une table de salle à manger orange au centre, deux escaliers de marbre baignés de lumière naturelle, un bureau sur mesure et, en général des espaces intéressants, aux proportions élégantes, en relation permanente avec l'extérieur.

Dieses Haus steht im Viertel Alto de Pinheiros in São Paulo. Diese Stadt ist, dem Architekten nach, vielleicht die hässlichste der ganzen Welt. Eine große weiße Umhüllung dient als Außenmauer und isoliert das Gebäude von der Umgebung, in der es sich befindet, um eine eigene Landschaft entstehen zu lassen, zu der es sich hinwenden kann. Die Kunden legten von Anfang an fest, was sie sich wünschten, ein riesiges Regal, das sich über das gesamte Wohnzimmer mit doppelter Höhe erstreckt, große Fenster, die sich zum Garten hin öffnen, einen Swimmingpool, eine Küche, in deren Mitte ein orangener Esstisch stehen sollte, zwei symmetrisch verlaufende Marmortreppen, auf die Tageslicht fällt, ein auf Maß gearbeitetes Atelier und im allgemeinen edle Räume in eleganten Proportionen, die ständig mit der Umgebung in Verbindung stehen sollten.

The shelves, which stretch to the double-height ceiling in the living room, illustrate the designers' intention to take full advantage of the dimensions of the structure.

Les étagères, qui s'élèvent jusqu'au toit du salon à double hauteur, reflètent l'intention d'optimiser les dimensions de la structure.

Mit den Regalen, die bis zur Decke des Wohnzimmers doppelter Höhe reichen, werden die Dimensionen der Struktur maximal ausgenutzt.

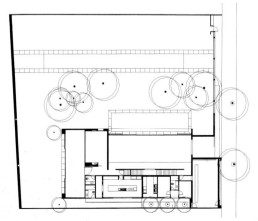

› Ground floor   Rez-de-chaussée   Erdgeschoss

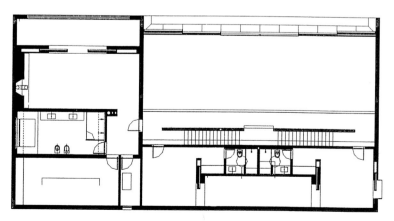

› First floor   Premier étage   Erstes Obergeschoss

The geometry of its shapes and the rational layout of its rooms transform this house into a refined architectural expression.

La géométrie des formes et la distribution rationnelle des espaces de vie, transforment cette habitation en une expression architecturale épurée.

Die Geometrie der Formen und die rationelle Verteilung der Räume macht dieses Haus zu einem bereinigten Ausdruck der Architektur.

Apartment in Wakayama
Appartement à Wakayama
Appartement in Wakayama

Wakayama, Japan

The design of this apartment turns the traditional concept of the "tsuboniwa" (small Japanese garden) on its end. Here, the architects subverted the traditional notion of the "tsuboniwa" by transforming it into a forbidden garden. While tradition holds that nature is introduced into buildings and then domesticated as a microcosm, here nature is abstracted, as symbolized by the lone tree that serves as a vertical element and the horizontal element represented by water. The water garden is the focal point of the house and can be seen from practically anywhere in the house. A path crosses it from one end to the other, as though it were floating on the tranquil surface of the pond. Steel, glass and pale colors highlight the austerity and Zen atmosphere of the house.

La conception de cet appartement tourne le dos au concept populaire de « tsuboniwa » (petit jardin japonais). Dans ce cas, les architectes ont remplacé la notion traditionnelle de « tsuboniwa » par celle d'un jardin interdit. Si d'ordinaire, la tradition veut que la nature s'introduise dans l'édifice et soit domestiquée en microcosmes, dans ce projet la nature est une abstraction symbolisée par un arbre solitaire en tant qu'élément vertical et par l'eau comme élément horizontal. Le jardin aquatique, point de mire de la maison, est visible de n'importe quel endroit à l'intérieur de la maison. Un chemin le traverse de part en part, comme s'il flottait au-dessus des eaux calmes. Acier, verre et tons clairs exaltent l'austérité et l'ambiance zen de l'habitation.

Bei der Gestaltung dieses Appartements verdrehte man das volkstümliche Konzept des "tsuboniwa" (kleiner japanischer Garten). In diesem Fall verwandelten die Architekten die traditionelle Vorstellung vom „tsuboniwa" in einen verbotenen Garten. Wenn es die Tradition verlangte, dass die Natur in das Gebäude mit einbezogen und in einem einzigen gebändigt wird, ist in diesem Gebäude die Natur eine Abstraktion, die von einem einsamen Baum als vertikalem Element und Wasser als horizontalem Element symbolisiert wird. Der Wassergarten ist der Mittelpunkt des Hauses und kann fast von jedem Raum aus gesehen werden. Ein Weg durchquert ihn von einem Ende zum anderen, so als ob er über der ruhigen Wasseroberfläche schweben würde. Stahl, Glas und helle Töne unterstreichen die Schlichtheit und die vom Zen-Buddhismus geprägte Atmosphäre des Hauses.

The design of this house – an abstraction of the traditional concept of the Japanese garden – is a mixture of modernity and tradition.

La conception de cette maison, idée abstraite du concept traditionnel de jardin japonais, conjugue modernité et tradition.

Die Gestaltung dieses Hauses, eine Abstraktion des traditionellen Konzeptes des japanischen Gartens, ist eine Vermischung von Modernität und Tradition.

The new aquatic garden is transformed into a forbidden space that can be admired from afar but remains off limits.

Le nouveau jardin aquatique se transforme en un espace interdit, créé uniquement pour le plaisir des yeux et non pour être emprunté.

Der neue Wassergarten wird zu einem verbotenen Raum, der nur betrachtet, aber nicht durchquert werden darf.

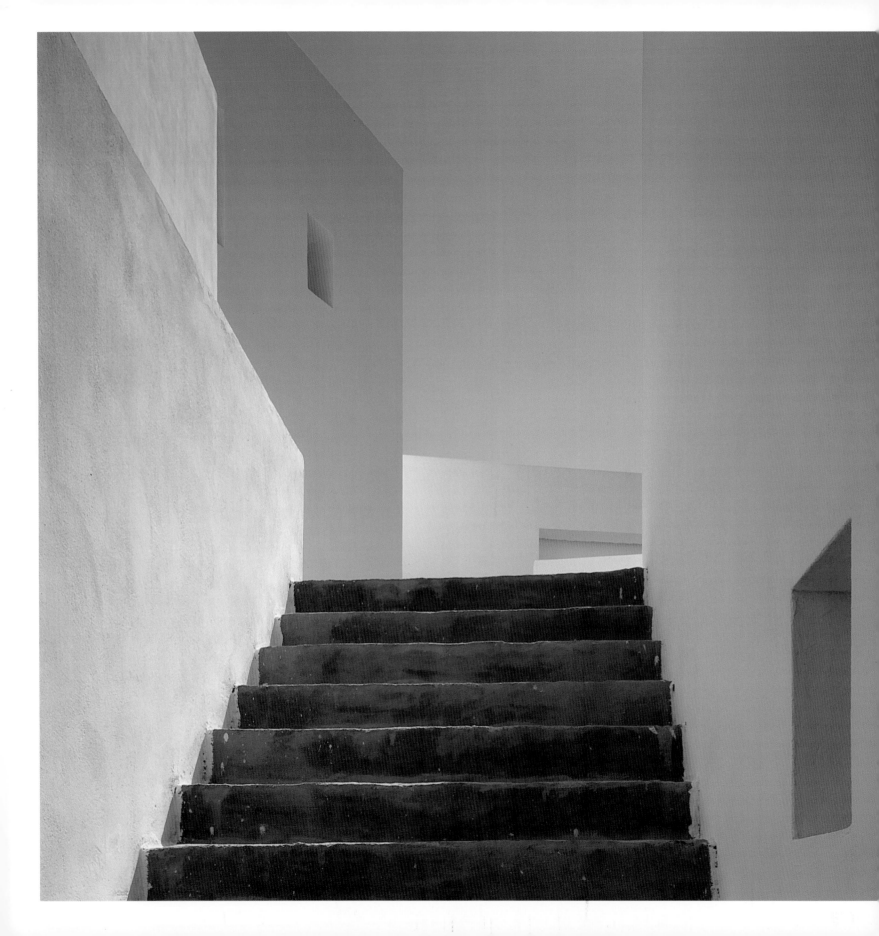

House in Milos
Maison à Milos
Haus in Milos

Milos, Greece

This house, situated on the edge of a cliff, 165 ft above the Aegean Sea in Crete, is the first and only building in the area. An apparently random distribution of volumes expresses flexibility and attempts to limit the impact of the house on the landscape. Each volume plays a specific role and possesses a unique geometry that forms part of a coherent design in the overall composition. The two structures located at the center of the dwelling contain the living room, kitchen and dining room, while the other holds independent bedrooms with private terraces. These autonomous rooms accentuate the sensation of tranquility and isolation that enhances the surroundings. The position of the volumes adapts to different activities and allows for an infinite number of configurations.

Cette maison située au bord d'une falaise, à 50 m au-dessus de la mer, en Crète, est la seule et unique construction aux alentours. La distribution des volumes, aléatoire en apparence, exprime la flexibilité et tend à limiter l'impact sur le paysage. Chaque volume a une fonction particulière et possède une géométrie unique faisant partie d'un design cohérent dans la composition des espaces. Les deux structures situées au centre hébergent le salon, la cuisine et la salle à manger, tandis que les autres accueillent des chambres indépendantes disposant de terrasses privées. Ces pièces autonomes accentuent la sensation de calme et d'isolement en exaltant la perception des alentours. L'emplacement des volumes s'adapte aux diverses activités et permet d'infinies configurations.

Dieses Haus steht am Rand einer Steilküste, 50 m über dem Meer von Kreta, und ist das erste und einzige Haus in dieser Zone. Die anscheinend zufällige Verteilung der Gebäudeteile wirkt flexibel und soll den Eingriff in die Landschaft verringern. Jeder Gebäudeteil erfüllt eine spezifische Funktion und besitzt eine einzigartige Geometrie, die Teil einer kohärenten Gestaltung der Räume ist. In den beiden Strukturen im Zentrum befinden sich das Wohnzimmer, die Küche und das Speisezimmer, in den anderen Strukturen liegen unabhängige Räume mit privaten Terrassen. Diese unabhängigen Räume unterstreichen den Eindruck von Ruhe und Einsamkeit und erhöhen die Wahrnehmung der Umgebung. Die Anordnung der Strukturen ist an verschiedene Aktivitäten angepasst und lässt zahlreiche Gestaltungsmöglichkeiten zu.

› **Ground floor** Rez-de-chaussée Erdgeschoss   › **First floor** Premier étage Erstes Obergeschoss   › **Second floor** Deuxième étage Zweites Obergeschoss

Na Xemena House
Habitation Na Xemena
Haus Na Xemena

Ibiza, Spain

From the moment the first plans were drafted and the range of materials and colors were chosen, the volumes and construction elements of this house conceived to express a great degree of fluidity. From the exterior, the arrangement of the terraces and the pool – slightly off kilter from one another – creates a visual perspective that leads the eye to the exact geometry of the volumes of the house. The outside walls – extremely pure and stripped of all ornamentation – were punctured with holes to capture light, in a manner designed to maintain the natural order established by the configuration of the interior. Here, filled spaces are decorated with colors obtained from natural pigments: gray on the floors and terraces, and indigo on the vertical planes. The walls – painted white and cobalt blue – constitute a unifying element throughout the house, and are further set off by being lit from above.

Dès les premières esquisses et après le choix initial des matériaux et des couleurs, les volumes et les éléments structuraux de cette habitation ont été conçus pour exprimer une grande fluidité. De l'extérieur, la disposition des terrasses et de la piscine à des niveaux différents, crée une perspective visuelle qui mène vers la géométrie parfaite des volumes de la maison. Les murs extérieurs, soignés et dénudés, ont été perforés pour capter la lumière selon un ordre naturel défini par la configuration intérieure, où les espaces pleins sont ornés de couleurs à base de pigments naturels, gris pour les sols et les terrasses, indigo pour les plans verticaux. Les murs -peints en blanc et bleu cobalt- mis en valeur par un éclairage zénithal, sont l'élément unificateur de la maison.

Schon als man mit der Planung begann und das Material auswählte, war der Grundgedanke für dieses Gebäude und die Konstruktionselemente immer, dass sie ein Fließen ausdrücken sollten. Bereits außen wird durch die Anordnung der Terrassen und des Swimmingpools mit leichten Höhenunterschieden eine visuelle Perspektive geschaffen, die zu der exakten Geometrie der Formen des Hauses führt. Die Außenmauern sind rein und nackt. Sie wurden durchbohrt, um das Licht einzufangen und in das Innere zu leiten, wo volle Räume dominieren, die mit Farben dekoriert sind, die aus natürlichen Pigmenten hergestellt wurden. Die Böden und Terrassen sind grau und die vertikalen Flächen indigoblau. Die Wände in weiß und kobaltblau, unterstrichen durch das Licht von oben, sind die Elemente, die das Haus vereinheitlichen.

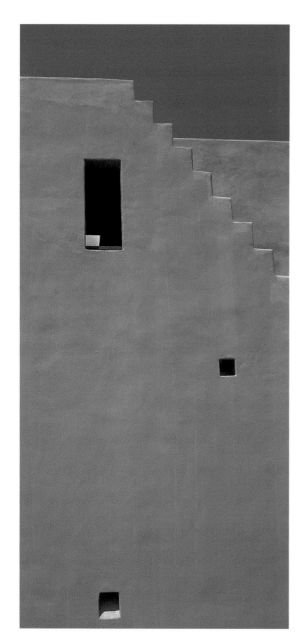

This compact and simple ensemble, built on a rocky outcrop, blends perfectly into the crags of the cliff.

L'ensemble compact et simple, construit sur une base rocheuse, s'intègre parfaitement au profil de la falaise.

Das kompakte und einfache Gebäude, das auf einem Untergrund aus Felsen errichtet wurde, fügt sich perfekt in die Geländeform der Steilküste ein.

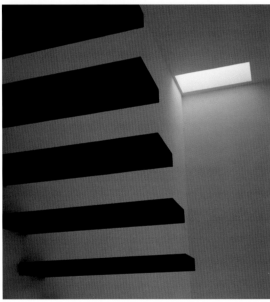

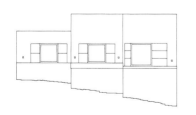

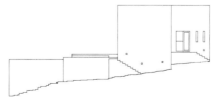

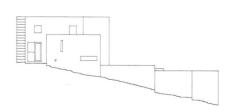

› Elevations Élévations Aufrisse

The ensemble aims to create a harmonious relationship with its surroundings, and a soft and logical transition between building and landscape.

L'ensemble aspire à une relation harmonieuse avec l'environnement, à une transition douce et logique entre construction et paysage.

Das Gebäude sollte sich harmonisch in die Umgebung einfügen, und es sollte einen sanften und logischen Übergang zwischen dem Bau und der Landschaft ergeben.

Residence in Ibiza
Résidence à Ibiza
Haus in Ibiza

Ibiza, Spain

This house represents the halfway point between a traditional building and a sophisticated contemporary residence. Its owner designed most of the elements that make up the building. The layout of the rooms was conventional: the lower floor contains the living areas and a guest bedroom, while the main bedroom is located on the upper floor. The perception of a division in space is achieved through the walls and the openings cut in them. Special attention was paid to the finishes of the surfaces, as the palettes of materials and colors were kept within certain limits. The floors are paved in stone – there are no tiles, not even in the bathrooms, where the floors are paved with rounded pebbles. The result is a coherent and refined project that integrates elements with a high degree of visual purity.

Cette résidence est à mi-chemin entre une construction traditionnelle et une habitation contemporaine sophistiquée. Le propriétaire a conçu la majorité des éléments qui constituent l'édifice. La distribution des pièces est conventionnelle : le rez-de-chaussée accueille les salons et une chambre d'amis, tandis que la pièce principale se trouve à l'étage supérieur. La division visuelle de l'espace se fait grâce à des murs et aux ouvertures qui y sont pratiquées. Une attention particulière a été accordée aux finitions et revêtements des surfaces, se limitant à une petite gamme de matériaux et à une modeste palette de couleurs. Les sols en pierre sont fluides, dépourvus de carrelage, même dans les salles de bains où les sols sont en galets. Le résultat d'ensemble est cohérent et épuré, intégrant des éléments d'une grande pureté visuelle.

Dieses Haus befindet sich auf halbem Weg zwischen der traditionellen Architektur und einem edlen, zeitgemäßen Gebäude. Der Eigentümer selbst entwarf die meisten Elemente, aus denen das Haus besteht. Die Verteilung der Zimmer ist konventionell, im Erdgeschoss befinden sich das Wohnzimmer und das Gästezimmer, und im Obergeschoss das Schlafzimmer. Die visuelle Unterteilung des Raumes erfolgte durch Wände und Öffnungen. Besonderer Wert wurde auf die Verkleidung der Oberflächen gelegt, für die nur eine kleine Auswahl an Materialien und Farben benutzt wurde. Die Böden sind durchgehend aus Stein. Es gibt keine Fliesen, nicht einmal in den Bädern. Dort bestehen die Böden aus Kieselsteinen. So entstand eine kohärente und klare Wohnumgebung, die Elemente mit einer großen visuellen Reinheit beinhaltet.

The rustic furnishings contrast with the simple and refined shapes of some of the structural elements, such as the fireplace in the living room.

Le mobilier rustique contraste avec les formes simples et raffinées de certains éléments structurels, à l'instar de la cheminée du salon.

Die rustikalen Möbel stehen zu den einfachen und edlen Formen einiger der Strukturelemente im Gegensatz, wie zum Beispiel dieser Kamin im Wohnzimmer.

A staircase leads from the living room to the bedrooms on the upper floor.

A partir du salon, un escalier conduit vers les chambres situées à l'étage supérieur.

Vom Wohnzimmer aus führt eine Treppe in die Schlafzimmer im Obergeschoss.

In the kitchen, the simple lines of the modern furniture coexist peacefully with rustic details.

Dans la cuisine, l'équipement moderne aux lignes simples côtoie des détails rustiques.

In der Küche teilt sich die moderne Ausstattung in einfachen Linien mit rustikalen Einzelheiten den Platz.

The bathroom is situated alongside the main bedroom, which is distinguished by a bed framed in a rectangular structure made of cement.

La salle de bains est située à côté de la chambre principale d'où se détache un lit délimité par une structure rectangulaire en ciment.

Das Bad liegt am Hauptschlafzimmer, dessen auffälligstes Element ein Bett ist, das von einer rechteckigen Zementstruktur gerahmt ist.

Here, the bed and the bathroom share a single space, in stripped of all doors.

Dans cette pièce à vivre, lit et salle de bains partagent le même espace dépourvu de portes.

In diesem Zimmer teilen sich Bett und Bad den Raum. Es gibt keine Türen.

House in Beijing
Habitation à Pékin
Haus in Peking

Beijing, China

KNTA Architects is one of the most renowned and representative firms in both Singapore and southeast Asia. According to the architects, this house was designed to blend perfectly into its natural surroundings and to respond to the needs and esthetic interests of its owners. The design comprises two L-shaped volumes – one larger than the other but attached to the first – which are carefully located in the natural contours of a valley to blend perfectly into the setting. The smaller volume, which contains the kitchen and dining room, faces the northern part of the valley and rests on the edge of a steep cliff. Its intersection at an angle of 45° is the site of the living quarters.

KNTA Architects est un des bureaux d'architecture les plus en vue et les plus connus à Singapour et à Otoda, la région du sud-est asiatique. Dans ce projet, les architectes ont conçu l'habitation pour l'intégrer parfaitement au paysage naturel et répondre aux besoins et intérêts esthétiques des propriétaires. La conception prévoit deux volumes en forme de L, l'un plus grand que l'au-tre, le plus petit étant adossé au premier, tous deux implantés délicatement dans le paysage naturel d'une vallée où ils s'intègrent à merveille. Le plus petit volume qui accueille la cuisine et la zone de la salle à manger, est tourné vers le nord de la vallée et repose au bord d'un précipice couvert de pins, formant un angle de 45° avec l'édifice principal, où se trouve l'espace réservé à la chambre.

KNTA Architects ist eines der wichtigsten und bekanntesten Architekturstudios in Singapur und Otoda in Südostasien. Dieses Haus wurde, wie die Architekten sagten, so entworfen, dass es sich perfekt in die umgebende Natur einfügt und allen Ansprüchen und ästhetischen Interessen der Eigentümer gerecht wird. Das Gebäude besteht aus zwei Teilen, die ein L bilden. Ein Teil ist größer, der andere kleiner und lehnt sich an den ersten an. Diese mit großer Sorgfalt entworfene Form fügt sich perfekt in das umgebende Tal ein. Im kleineren Gebäudeteil befinden sich die Küche und das Speisezimmer. Er zeigt zum Norden des Tales und liegt an einem steilen Abgrund. Der Winkel zwischen diesem Gebäudeteil und dem Hauptgebäude, in dem sich die Wohnräume befinden, beträgt 45°.

The details of the building were carefully planned throughout the house. The living room is distinguished by its fireplace, which is a cubic structure in the middle of an open space.

Cette habitation a été étudiée dans les moindres détails architecturaux. Au salon, la cheminée placée au cœur de l'espace, est mise en valeur, à l'instar d'une sculpture cubique.

Alle Konstruktionselemente des Hauses wurden mit großer Sorgfalt behandelt. Im Wohnzimmer hebt sich der Kamin ab, der wie eine kubische Skulptur mitten im Raum wirkt.

The expressiveness of the natural light bathes the living room in a constantly changing array of colours.

L'expressivité de la lumière naturelle inonde le salone de tonalités toujours différentes.

Die Ausdrucksstärke des Tageslichtes färbt das Wohnzimmer immer wieder in anderen Tönen.

Apartment N
Appartement N
Appartement N

Cuneo, Italy

This design aimed to transmit an image that reflected its owner's commitment with the world of art. To do this, the architects studied the quality of the space and came to the conclusion that they would have to make the most of the constructed surface area. This entailed creating a simple but bright path through the building, which would guarantee views of the artworks from any given point in the house. Once the distribution of functions had been decided, a white rectangular module was designed to frame one of the best pieces in the collection. From the spacious dining room – a veritable art gallery in its own right – this piece can be observed by guests sitting in any of the comfortable armchairs. The architects thus created a space in which the only visual obstacle is an element that sets off a work of art.

Ce projet cherche à transmettre une image fidèle à la relation que le propriétaire entretient avec l'art. Pour cela, les architectes après avoir étudié les qualités spatiales, ont décidé de rentabiliser au maximum la surface construite pour créer un espace simple et diaphane, garantissant la vue des œuvres d'art depuis n'importe quel endroit de la maison. Une fois les fonctions distribuées, les architectes ont conçu un module rectangulaire blanc, servant de cadre à l'une des plus belles œuvres de la collection : depuis la vaste salle à manger, véritable galerie d'art, il est possible de la contempler assis sur un fauteuil confortable. Les maîtres d'œuvre ont pu ainsi réaliser un espace où l'unique obstacle visuel est un élément qui sublime l'art.

Die Gestaltung dieser Wohnung sollte das Interesse des Eigentümers für die Kunst ausdrücken. Dazu haben die Architekten die Eigenschaften des Raums analysiert und kamen zu dem Schluss, dass die bebaute Oberfläche so stark wie möglich rentabilisiert werden musste. Es sollte ein einfacher und transparenter Flur entstehen, der die Sichtbarkeit der Kunstwerke von jedem Punkt des Hauses aus garantiert. Nach Verteilung der verschiedenen Raumfunktionen wurde ein rechteckiges, weißes Modul entworfen, das als Rahmen für eines der besten Stücke der Sammlung dient. Dieses Werk kann man von dem großen Wohnzimmer aus, das wie eine Kunstgalerie wirkt, auf einem bequemen Sessel sitzend betrachten. So haben die Architekten einen Raum entworfen, in dem das einzige visuelle Hindernis ein Element ist, das die Kunst umrahmt.

The only boundary separating the dining room from the living area is the rectangular module that frames the main piece in the collection.

La seule séparation entre la salle à manger et le salon est un module rectangulaire qui met en valeur l'œuvre essentielle de la collection.

Die einzige Begrenzung, die das Speisezimmer vom Wohnzimmer trennt, ist das rechteckige Modul, das das wichtigste Werk der Sammlung umrahmt.

› Plan Plan Grundriss

Type/Variant House
Maison Type/Variant
Haus Type/Variant

Wisconsin, USA

This house is a composition of different volumes that differentiate themselves both in their proportions as well as through their orientation; so, natural light always enters each of them in a unique way. According to the architect, the house was designed to reflect the rhythm of life, so, changes in its circumstances should be reflected in the composition itself. The result is a house that plays with angles of vision and creates different orientations, while the variation in heights creates a dynamic interior. The domestic activities take place indoors as well as on the outdoor terraces located in the center of each structure. Outside, a range of different materials was to bring to life various themes that would confer rhythm on the design and that would convey the emotions sought by its creator.

Cette habitation est composée de différents volumes qui se différencient tant par les dimensions que par l'orientation, en fonction des variations de la lumière naturelle qui les parcourent. Selon l'architecte, la maison doit refléter le rythme de la vie et ses modulations doivent être intégrées à la composition architecturale. Il en résulte une construction qui joue avec les angles de vision, créant différentes orientations, pendant que les variations de hauteur à l'intérieur imprègnent l'ensemble d'un puissant dynamisme. Les activités familiales se déroulent à l'intérieur et sur les terrasses extérieures situées au sein de chaque structure. A l'extérieur, la disposition des divers matériaux s'inscrit dans une gamme de motifs variés qui rythme le projet et lui confère l'émotion requise.

Dieses Haus besteht aus einer Komposition verschiedener Teile, die sowohl in Proportion als auch in ihrer Himmelsrichtung völlig unterschiedlich sind, so dass der Lichteinfall in diese Gebäudeteile sehr unterschiedlich ist. Der Architekt sagte, dass das Haus den Lebensrhythmus widerspiegeln soll und die Veränderungen sollten sich in die architektonische Komposition integrieren. Das Ergebnis ist ein Gebäude, das mit den Sichtwinkeln spielt und verschiedene Ausrichtungen schafft. Durch die Höhenunterschiede im Inneren wirkt das Gesamtgebäude sehr dynamisch. Die häuslichen Aktivitäten finden in den Räumen und den Terrassen im Freien statt, die sich im Zentrum jeder Struktur befinden. Im Außenbereich sind verschiedene Materialien nach verschiedenen Entwürfen angeordnet, so dass sie dem Haus einen Rhythmus geben und die Emotion vermitteln, die gesucht wurde.

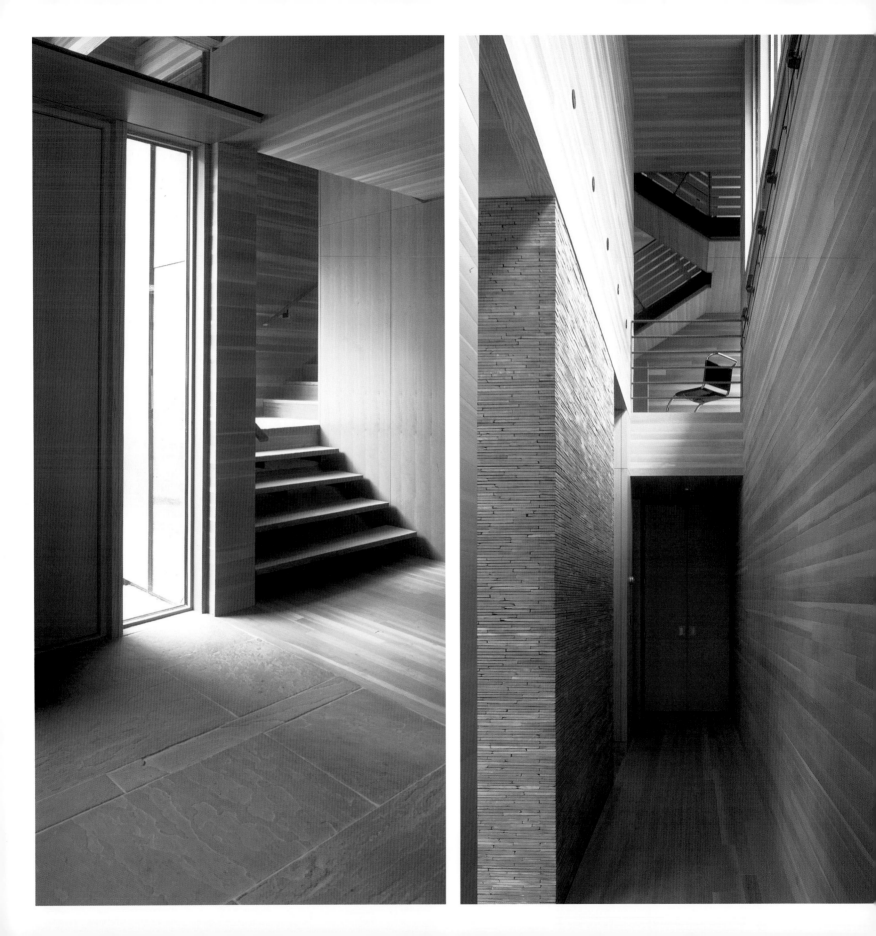

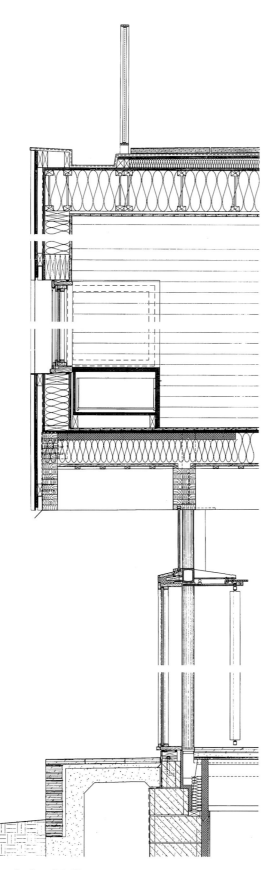

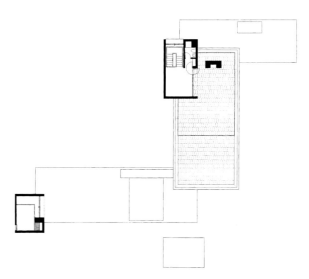

› Second floor Deuxième étage Zweites Obergeschoss

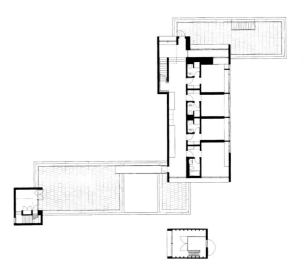

› First floor Premier étage Erstes Obergeschoss

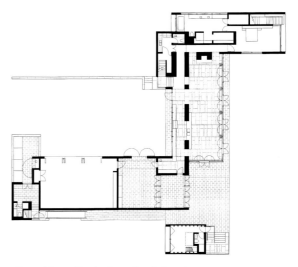

› Section Section Schnitt

232

› Ground floor Rez-de-chaussée Erdgeschoss

Divided house
Maison séparée
Geteiltes Haus

Beijing, China

This house, as its name suggests, is divided into two halves, in order to create a range of angles and spaces and blend into its mountainous surroundings. With a design that adapts to the topography of the site, the two highly adaptable wings of the house rotate 360° around themselves and adapt to the surrounding terrain. The house was built with an environmentally-friendly wooden and earth structure that aimed to respect traditional Chinese architecture as deeply as possible, but without resorting to mimicry. This is instead an attempt at creating a new architectural vision for a new China. Inside, one's eyes catch a glimpse of a freestanding wooden staircase that leads to the top floor and echoes the effect of the sequence of beams in the ceiling.

La maison séparée est, comme son nom l'indique, divisée en deux moitiés pour créer divers angles et espaces et s'intégrer à la région montagneuse où elle se trouve. Modulables à souhait et fortes d'une conception parfaitement adaptée à la topographie, les deux ailes de la maison peuvent pivoter sur elles-mêmes à 360° et s'adapter au terrain environnant. La maison possède une structure écologique composée de bois et de terre, essayant de respecter le plus possible la tradition architecturale chinoise sans en être pour autant une pure reproduction. Il s'agit plutôt d'une tentative de créer une nouvelle vision architecturale pour une Chine nouvelle. A l'intérieur, un escalier de bois se détache, sans contremarche, s'élevant jusqu'au niveau supérieur, reproduisant l'effet créé par l'enfilade de poutres du toit.

Das geteilte Haus ist, wie sein Name schon sagt, in zwei Hälften geteilt, um verschiedene Winkel und Räume zu schaffen, die sich in das Berggebiet integrieren, in dem das Haus liegt. Das Haus ist sehr vielseitig und seine Form ahmt die Bodenform nach. Die beiden Flügel können über sich selbst bis zu 360° gedreht und an das umgebende Gelände angepasst werden. Das Haus hat ein ökologischen Skelett aus Holz und Erde und man versuchte, so weit wie möglich die chinesische Tradition zu berücksichtigen, ohne sie jedoch nachzuahmen. Es wurde versucht, eine neue architektonische Vision für das neue China zu schaffen. Im Inneren fällt vor allem eine Holztreppe ohne Setzstufen auf, die bis in das obere Stockwerk führt und die Wirkung einer Reihe von Dachbalken nachahmt.

A translucent screen filters the light that penetrates into the interior and serves to separate the different areas.

Un paravent translucide filtre la lumière qui pénètre à l'intérieur, agissant en élément séparateur des différents espaces de vie.

Durch einen lichtdurchlässigen Schirm fällt Licht in das Innere und er dient als Trennelement zwischen den verschiedenen Bereichen.

The opaque materials of the exterior blend effortlessly with the transparent finishes of the interior.

Les matériaux opaques de l'extérieur se marient à la transparence des finitions intérieures.

Die lichtundurchlässigen Materialien außen werden mit der Transparenz der Oberflächen innen kombiniert.

The warm wooden walls of the bedroom contrast with the cold finishes in the bathroom.

La chaleur du revêtement de bois dans la chambre à coucher contraste avec la froideur des finitions de la salle de bains.

Die warm wirkende Holzverkleidung im Schlafzimmer steht zu den kalten Oberflächen im Bad im Gegensatz.

Duplex in Legnano
Duplex à Legnano
Duplex in Legnano

Legnano, Italy

The project to renovate this house, originally restored in 1950, involved building two new stories on top of the existing two levels. This approach was made possible by the flat roof. The new structure, which contrasts with the existing building, rises up as a steel structure that gives way to two completely open and transparent new stories. The exterior façade, which maintains some of the traditional details, extends to the cornice of the neighboring building. A stairway connects all the floors in the building and is the only structural element linking the old and the new. The ground floor, designed as a large, elongated space, contains the daytime areas and includes a living room, kitchen and dining room. The upper floor contains a bright bedroom that benefits from the natural light filtering in through a skylight.

Le projet de réhabilitation de cette maison, restaurée en 1950, est basé sur la construction de deux nouveaux étages sur les deux niveaux existants : réalisation rendue possible grâce à la disposition horizontale du toit. La nouvelle structure, contrastant avec la construction antérieure, s'élève sur un squelette d'acier sur deux niveaux entièrement ouverts et transparents. La façade extérieure, qui a conservé certains détails du style traditionnel, s'étend jusqu'à la corniche de l'édifice limitrophe. Un escalier relie tous les niveaux des étages de l'édifice et reste le seul élément structurel qui relie les deux constructions. Le rez-de-chaussée, conçu comme un vaste espace tout en longueur, accueille la zone de jour comprenant salon, cuisine et salle à manger. A l'étage supérieur, la chambre est diaphane, bénéficiant de la lumière naturelle filtrée par le velux.

Dieses project, das 1950 renoviert wurde, sollte auf den beiden existierenden Ebenen um zwei neue Stockwerke erweitert werden. Dies war durch die horizontale Anordnung des Daches möglich. Die neue Struktur, die im Gegensatz zu der bereits vorhandenen steht, erhebt sich auf einem Stahlskelett mit zwei absolut offenen und transparenten Ebenen. An der Fassade zur Straße hat man unterschiedliche Einzelheiten des traditionellen Stils beibehalten. Sie reicht bis zur Deckenleiste des angrenzenden Hauses. Eine Treppe verbindet alle Stockwerke des Gebäudes. Sie ist das einzige Strukturelement, das beide Konstruktionen verbindet. Im Erdgeschoss befindet sich ein großer, langer Raum, in dem das Wohnzimmer, die Küche und das Speisezimmer untergebracht sind. Im Obergeschoss liegt ein transparentes Schlafzimmer, in das reichlich Tageslicht durch ein Dachfenster fällt.

The two new floors rise up like a transparent container on the top of the original structure.

Les deux étages nouvellement construits s'élèvent, à l'instar d'un container transparent, au-dessus de la structure préexistante.

Die beiden Stockwerke des Neubaus erheben sich, an einen transparenten Container erinnernd, auf der Struktur, die bereits existierte.

The light that filters in through the skylight guarantees the luminosity of this bright and uncluttered space.

La lumière, filtrée par le velux, illumine cet espace diaphane, paré d'un minimum d'éléments.

Das Licht, das durch das Dachfenster fällt, lässt den mit wenig Elementen dekorierten Raum hell und transparent wirken.

The stairway, with its wooden treads and steel structure, is the only element that connects the two levels of the building.

L'escalier, aux marches de bois et à la structure d'acier, est le seul élément qui relie les deux niveaux de l'édifice.

Die Treppe mit ihren Holzstufen und der Stahlstruktur ist das einzige Element, das die beiden Ebenen der Wohnung verbindet.

Apartment in Knokke
Appartement à Knokke
Appartement in Knokke

Knokke, Belgium

This two-story apartment possesses a number of terraces that offer breathtaking views out to sea. The main idea was to create a means of access from the elevator and the indoor stairways located in the central area of the house – and in doing so, to eliminate the need for vertical divisions. Large windows were opened on to the interior, thereby not only satisfying the demand for natural light but also providing pleasant views of the surrounding area. The layout of the upper level follows the same scheme, with spaces distributed around a central nucleus and no vertical dividers. The bedrooms, however, can be divided or joined by means of sliding doors, thus ensuring privacy. Some materials, such as the dark stone used in some areas, were selected to lend a air of solidity and stability to the ensemble.

Cet appartement de deux étages est doté de diverses terrasses offrant des vues extraordinaires sur la mer. L'idée principale réside dans la création d'accès depuis l'ascenseur et les intérieurs situés dans la zone centrale de l'édifice, supprimant ainsi la nécessité d'avoir recours à des cloisons verticales. De vastes fenêtres s'ouvrent sur l'intérieur, permettant de diffuser la lumière naturelle et par la même, de jouir de la beauté des vues ainsi offertes. L'étage supérieur suit le même schéma de distribution spatiale à savoir, l'absence de cloisons autour d'un noyau central. Par contre, dans les chambres à coucher, il est possible de diviser ou d'unifier l'espace grâce à des portes coulissantes, assurant l'intimité requise. Certains matériaux, à l'instar de la pierre sombre utilisée dans certaines zones, ont été choisis pour conférer à l'ensemble une image de solidité et de stabilité.

Diese zweistöckige Wohnung hat mehrere Terrassen, von denen man einen ausgezeichneten Blick aufs Meer hat. Die grundlegende Idee der Planer war es, vom Fahrstuhl und von den inneren Treppen in der Mitte des Gebäudes aus Zugänge zu schaffen und so die vertikalen Trennelemente eliminieren zu können. Große Fenster öffnen sich nach innen und lassen viel Licht ein. Außerdem lassen sie den schönen Blick frei. In der oberen Etage sind die Räume ebenfalls um einen zentralen Kern verteilt. Die Schlafzimmer können jedoch durch Schiebetüren geöffnet oder abgetrennt werden, und, falls gewünscht, für mehr Intimsphäre sorgen. Manche der Materialien, wie der dunkle Stein in einigen Räumen, wurden gewählt, um das Gebäude solide und zusammenhängend wirken zu lassen.

The various areas are organized sequentially and arranged around a central nucleus.

Les différents espaces sont organisés en enfilade et disposés autour d'un noyau central.

Die verschiedenen Bereiche sind in Sequenzen angelegt und um einen zentralen Kern herum angeordnet.

House in Gloucestershire
Habitation dans le Gloucestershire
Haus in Gloucestershire

Gloucestershire, UK

This house, with its Palladian façade, was built at the turn of the 20th century. In the 1920s, however, the original ballroom was converted into a set of low-ceilinged bedrooms. In the most recent renovation, these volumes were reorganized to create different areas that comprise a house with one living room, one bathroom, a bedroom and a small dressing room. To return the building to its original state, the ceilings were raised, the chimney flues were torn out and the windows were brought back to their original size. Inside, three architectural elements were inserted perpendicular to the main axis of the house, to divide it into four areas. These elements can also be used as furniture.

Cet édifice à la façade palladienne a été construit au début du siècle passé. Au cours des années 20, l'ancienne salle de danse a été restructurée en de plus petits espaces recouverts d'un toit peu élevé. Lors de la dernière restauration, le volume a été redistribué pour créer différentes zones constituant une habitation individuelle avec un salon, une salle de bains, une chambre à coucher et une petite pièce servant éventuellement de dressing. Pour redonner à l'édifice son aspect original, les toits ont été relevés, les conduits de cheminées démolis et les fenêtres élargies. A l'intérieur, trois éléments architecturaux ont été construits, disposés perpendiculairement à l'axe principal de l'habitation qu'ils divisent en quatre sphères. Qui plus est, ils peuvent servir de meubles.

Dieses Gebäude mit seiner palladianischen Fassade wurde Anfang des vergangenen Jahrhunderts errichtet. In den Zwanzigerjahren strukturierte man den ehemaligen Tanzsaal um, um daraus kleine Zimmer mit niedrigen Decken zu machen. Während der letzten Renovierung wurden die Räume wieder umgestaltet, um verschiedene Bereiche zu schaffen, die eine individuelle Wohnung mit einem Wohnzimmer, einem Bad, einem Schlafzimmer und einem kleinen Ankleidezimmer bilden. Um dem Gebäude sein Originalaussehen wieder zu geben, wurden die Decken erhöht, die Kaminrohre entfernt und die Fenster vergrößert. Im Inneren wurden drei architektonische Elemente geschaffen, die senkrecht zu Hauptachse der Wohnung angebracht sind und sie in vier Bereiche teilen. Außerdem kann man diese Elemente als Möbel benutzen.

Light, easy-to-maneuver materials were used for the modules that divide the interior.

Les modules divisant l'espace intérieur ont été réalisés en matériaux légers pour faciliter la construction.

Für die Module, die die Innenräume teilen, wurden leichte Materialien gewählt, die einfach zu verarbeiten sind.

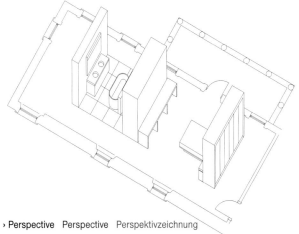

› Perspective Perspective Perspektivzeichnung

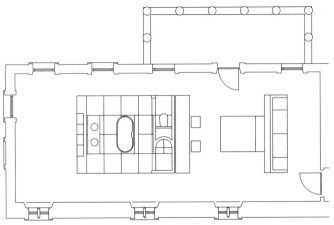

› Plan   Plan   Grundriss

The dark wood of the furniture contrasts with the color of the original parquet floor of the house.

Les meubles, en bois sombre, contrastent avec le sol qui a gardé la couleur du parquet d'origine de la maison.

Die Möbel aus dunklem Holz bilden einen Konstrast zu dem Boden, der die Farbe des Originalparketts des Hauses hat.

Loft H

New York, USA

One of the main requirements of the owner of this loft was to create an oasis amidst the bustle of New York. To unify the design and create a comfortable and austere atmosphere, the architect Kar-Hwa Ho decided to create a coherent space that would pay special attention to the textures of details, using a limited range of materials and a thoughtful selection of finishes. The lighting helps to define the sequence of spaces and the dimensions of the ensemble. On the north façade, a row of windows provides spatial continuity to the bedrooms. This sensation is accentuated by the contrast between the dark wood floor and the pale colors of the finishes.

La principale exigence du propriétaire de ce loft était de créer une oasis au cœur de l'agitation de la ville de New York. Afin de réaliser une conception harmonieuse et un environnement confortable et sobre, l'architecte Kar-Hwa Ho a créé un espace cohérent et serein, accordant une attention toute particulière à la texture des détails constructifs, avec une palette de matériaux restreinte et une sélection de revêtements limitée. L'éclairage permet de définir l'enchaînement des espaces et la dimension de l'ensemble. Sur la façade nord, une enfilade de fenêtres confère aux chambres une certaine continuité, une sensation accentuée par le contraste entre la couleur sombre du bois utilisé sur le sol et les couleurs pâles des finitions.

Der Eigentümer dieses Lofts verspürte vor allem den Wunsch, eine Oase inmitten der hektischen Stadt New York zu schaffen. Um die Gestaltung zu vereinheitlichen und eine komfortable und nüchterne Umgebung zu schaffen, schuf der Architekt Kar-Hwa Ho einen kohärenten und ruhigen Raum. Besondere Aufmerksamkeit richtete er auf die Textur der konstruktiven Einzelheiten. Es wurden nur wenige Materialien eingesetzt und auch die Oberflächen sind sorgfältig ausgewählt. Die Beleuchtung definiert eine Reihe von Räumen und die Dimension der ganzen Wohnung. An der Nordfassade verleiht eine Reihe von Fenstern den Zimmern eine räumliche Kontinuität. Dieses Gefühl wird noch durch den Kontrast zwischen dem dunklen Holz der Böden und den blassen Farben der Oberflächen verstärkt.

The chairs and couch are upholstered in silk and mohair; their equisite delicacy blends effortlessly with the elegance of the other materials.

Les fauteuils et les sofas sont habillés de soie et de mohair. La délicatesse de ces tissus se marie à l'élégance du reste des matériaux.

Die Sessel und Sofas sind mit Seide und Mohair bezogen. Diese feinen Stoffe passen gut zu der Eleganz der übrigen Materialien.

The spacious living room achieves the peace and purity sought by the architect.

L'immense salon reflète la sérénité et la pureté recherchées par l'architecte.

Das weiträumige Wohnzimmer wirkt ruhig und rein, so wie es der Architekt wünschte.

› Plan Plan Grundriss

The combination of colors and materials is repeated to lend continuity to the different areas in the house.

Le mélange des couleurs et des matériaux se répète pour créer une continuité entre les différents espaces.

Die Kombination der Farben und Materialien wird wiederholt, um eine Kontinuität zwischen den verschiedenen Bereichen zu schaffen.

New York, USA

Loft Giobbi-Valentino

This home, which serves as both a house and studio, is located in what was once a garment factory. To resolve what was a relatively complex structure, and to allow a degree of flexibility in the layout of the interiors, a system of panels was created; these serve multiple functions and are used as dividers, shelves and even lighting sources. The materials used to build these mobile, lightweight and translucent walls are highly flexible, allowing natural light to filter through. The same materials were used in the kitchen decor, though – in keeping with the overall aesthetic of the house – hand-polished concrete was chosen for the work surfaces.

Cette résidence, qui comporte un double programme d'habitation et de studio, se trouve dans une ancienne usine de vêtement. Pour parer à une structure relativement complexe et permettre une certaine flexibilité dans la disposition des intérieurs, le concepteur à créé un système de panneaux translucides à fonctions multiples, utilisés comme éléments de partition ou rayonnages et même comme source d'éclairage. Les matériaux utilisés pour ces murs amovibles, légers et translucides, permettent une grande flexibilité et laissent passer la lumière naturelle. Les mêmes matériaux ont été employés pour les meubles de la cuisine, mais c'est le béton banché et poli à la main qui a été retenu pour le revêtement, en harmonie avec l'esthétique générale de l'habitation.

Dieses Loft dient gleichzeitig als Wohnung und als Büro, und befindet sich in einer ehemaligen Textilfabrik. Um eine Lösung für die sehr komplexe Struktur zu finden und eine gewisse Flexibilität in der Anordnung der Räume zu ermöglichen, wurde ein System mit lichtdurchlässigen Paneelen geschaffen, das verschiedene Funktionen hat und als Trennelement, als Regal oder sogar als Lichtquelle benutzt werden kann. Die Materialien, aus denen diese beweglichen Wände konstruiert wurden, sind leicht und lichtdurchlässig. So sind sie sehr flexibel und lassen das Tageslicht durch. Die gleichen Materialien wurden für die Küchenmöbel verwendet, nur die Arbeitsfläche wurde vor Ort aus Beton gegossen und von Hand poliert. So passt sie gut zur allgemeinen Ästhetik der Wohnung.

In the kitchen, the few wooden elements contrast with the predominance of whites and metal finishes.

Dans la cuisine, les rares éléments de bois contrastent avec la prédominance du blanc et des finitions en métal.

In der Küche gibt es einige wenige Elemente aus Holz, die einen Kontrast zu der vorherrschenden Farbe Weiß und den Metalloberflächen bilden.

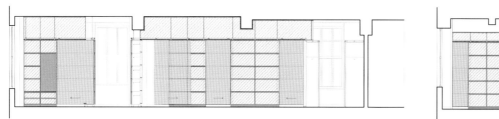

› **Cross section**   Section transversale   Querschnitt

Bamboo House
Maison de bambou
Bambushaus

Beijing, China

This house was designed by Japanese architect Kengo Kuma for the project "The Commune by the Great Wall". The aim was to study the formal characteristics of the Great Wall of China, as well as to present a selection of the work of best Asian architects. This project – one of the many that make up the Commune – criticizes the conventional forms produced by architecture, which often result in elements that have little to do with their surroundings. Here, the distinguishing properties and characteristics of the Great Wall are echoed by a lightweight but strong structure made of bamboo, which is of great cultural significance in both China and Japan.

Ce pavillon a été conçu par l'architecte japonais Kengo Kuma pour le projet « The Commune by The Great Wall » (La communauté à côté de la Grande Muraille) dont l'objectif est d'étudier les caractéristiques formelles de la Muraille et de créer un échantillon d'architecture des meilleurs architectes asiatiques. Ce projet, entre tous ceux qui forment le groupe de maisons de la communauté, masque une critique des formes conventionnelles de l'architecture qui produit très souvent des objets non intégrés à l'environnement. Ici les propriétés et les caractéristiques qui ressortent de la Grande Muraille s'expriment par le biais d'une structure légère et résistante en bambou, en hommage, aussi, à l'importante valeur culturelle que représente cette canne tant en Chine qu'au Japon.

Dieses Landhaus wurde von dem japanischen Architekten Kengo Kuma für das Projekt „The Commune by The Great Wall" (Die Gemeinschaft an der Großen Mauer) entworfen, dessen Ziel es war, die formellen Charakteristika der Chinesischen Mauer zu analysieren, und eine Ausstellung der besten asiatischen Architekten zu organisieren. Mit diesem Projekt, eines unter vielen in der Gruppe der Häuser der Gemeinschaft, wird eine verschleierte Kritik der konventionellen Formen der Architektur ausgedrückt, durch die oft Objekte entstehen, die nicht in ihre Umgebung passen. In diesem Haus werden die auffallenden Eigenschaften der Chinesischen Mauer durch eine leichte und widerstandsfähige Bambusstruktur ausgedrückt, die auch den großen kulturellen Wert zeigen soll, den der Bambus in China und in Japan hat.

The building's bamboo skeleton is clearly visible in the interior.

De l'intérieur on aperçoit le squelette de l'édifice formé par les cannes de bambou.

Im Inneren kann man das Skelett des Gebäudes aus Bambusrohr erkennen.

The interplay between bamboo canes is copied in the walls that outline the spaces and allow light to filter in.

Le jeu des cannes se reproduit sur les murs qui délimitent les espaces et filtrent la lumière.

Das Spiel mit dem Bambus wird in den Wänden wiederholt, die die Räume begrenzen und Licht einfallen lassen.

Inside, an extreme visual order is achieved through the absence of furniture, as this would disrupt the fluidity of the overall design.

A l'intérieur, un ordre visuel extrême règne grâce à l'absence de mobilier qui pourrait enfreindre la fluidité de l'ensemble.

Im Inneren wurde eine große, visuelle Ordnung erzielt, da es keine Möbel gibt, die das Fließen des Raumes behindern.

U&U House
Habitation U&U
Haus U&U

Tokyo, Japan

The uniqueness of the U&U House lies in the eight large shelves clad in plywood, which were expressly designed to hold the book collectionof the owners (a couple with one child). The shelves contribute to the fluidity of the space and simultaneously serve as dividers. As the site was located at the end of a cul-de-sac, the architect designed a terrace on the opposite end to obtain greater visual depth. The two spaces are separated by a sliding glass door; this allows light into both areas and adds to the impression of uniformity created by the wooden floor laid in all the rooms.

La singularité de la maison U&U réside dans les huit grandes étagères revêtues de couches de contreplaqué de bois conçues exprès pour accueillir l'immense collection de livres des propriétaires, une famille composée d'un couple et d'un enfant. Les étagères contribuent à la fluidité de l'espace tout en jouant le rôle de partition. La maison étant située dans une rue sans issue, l'architecte a conçu, de ce côté, une terrasse pour obtenir une plus grande profondeur visuelle. Une porte coulissante de verre sépare les deux espaces permettant à la lumière de parcourir les deux zones. Le revêtement en bois naturel de toutes les pièces accentue l'impression d'uniformité.

Was das Haus U&U so einzigartig macht, sind acht große Regale, die mit Holzfurnier verkleidet sind und in denen die große Bibliothek der Eigentümer untergebracht ist, ein Paar mit einem Kind. Die Regale tragen zu der Kontinuität des Raumes bei und erfüllen gleichzeitig die Funktion einer Trennwand. Das Grundstück liegt günstig in einer Sackgasse, so dass der Architekt auf der Seite, auf der die Straße endet, eine Terrasse anlegte, um mehr visuelle Tiefe zu erreichen. Die beiden Räume werden durch eine Schiebetür aus Glas getrennt, so dass Licht in beide Bereiche einfällt. Der Bodenbelag aus echtem Holz in allen Räumen lässt die Wohnumgebung einheitlich wirken.

Wood plays an important role throughout the house, as evident in the shelves, floor and furniture.

Le bois joue un rôle déterminant dans l'habitation comme le montrent l'étagère, le sol ou le mobilier.

Holz spielt eine wichtige Rolle in dieser Wohnung, was man sowohl an dem Regal als auch am Boden und den Möbeln erkennen kann.

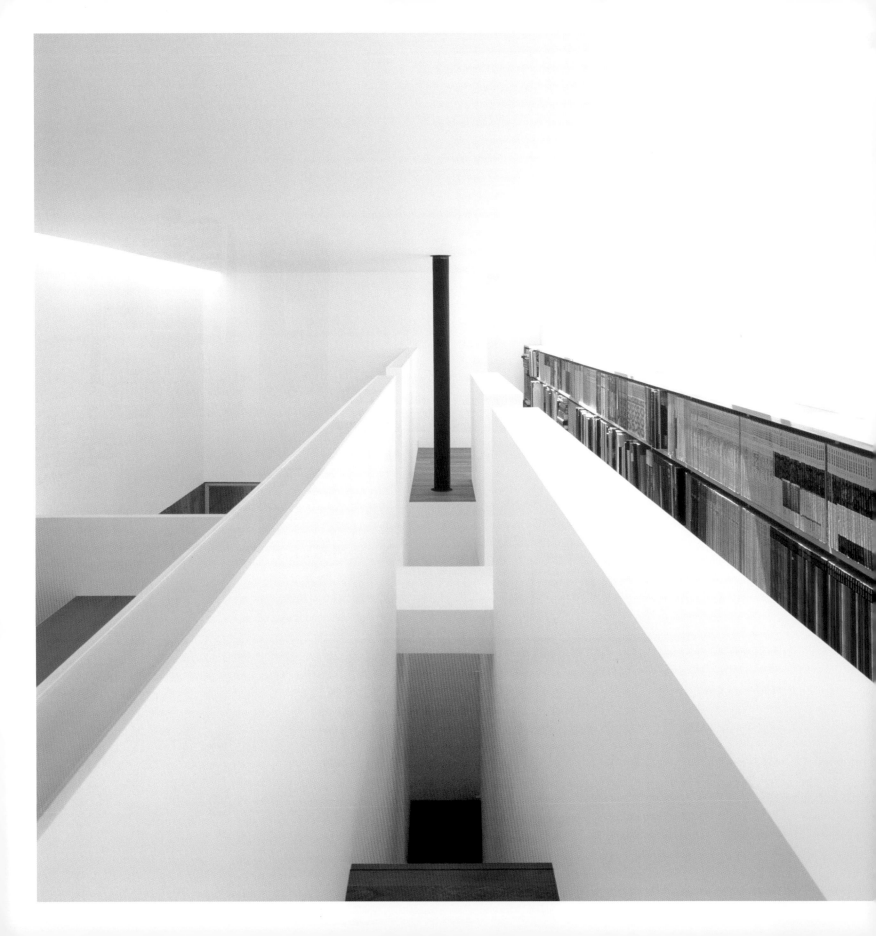

Diaphanous workshop
Atelier diaphane
Transparente Werkstatt

Osaka, Japan

Created as a horizontal grid that would work its way sinuously towards the sky, the interior of this house rises upwards by means of the stairway that connects it to the highest part of the building. The distribution of the walls was intended to create different spaces in which light enters at varying intensities, depending on the position of the sun. The interplay between the light and the resulting setting allows for a range of sensations that are only made possible by the skylight in the upper level or the fiber framework that defines the staircase area. Light descends through the skylight and filters through the main roof opening. Through this design, the architect allows the light that fills the space to become the primary element of the project.

Créé à l'instar d'un réticule horizontal qui s'élève en ondulant vers le ciel, l'intérieur s'érige à la verticale grâce aux escaliers qui communiquent avec la zone la plus haute de l'édifice. La disposition des murs crée divers espaces où l'intensité de la lumière diffère selon la position du soleil. Ce jeu relationnel entre la position du soleil et son incidence sur l'espace permet de créer un univers de sensations, impossible sans le velux supérieur, ni sans le treillis de fibres qui constitue l'espace de l'escalier. La lumière descend au travers du velux et est canalisée par l'ouverture centrale de la couverture. Grâce à cette conception, l'architecte parvient à ce que l'éclairage qui inonde l'espace, devienne le metteur en scène de l'espace en captant l'essence du projet.

Das Gebäude ist wie ein horizontales Raster angelegt, das sich kurvig in den Himmel streckt. Die Innenräume steigen über eine Treppe, die zum obersten Geschoss des Gebäudes führt, vertikal auf. Die Wände sind so verteilt, dass verschiedene Räume entstanden sind, in denen das Licht in verschiedenen Stärken je nach Sonnenstand einfällt. Durch dieses Spiel mit der Beziehung zwischen dem Sonnenstand und dem Lichteinfall entsteht eine Welt von Eindrücken, die ohne das Dachfenster und die verflochtenen Fasern der Treppen nicht möglich wäre. Das Licht fällt durch das Dachfenster ein und wird durch die zentrale Öffnung in der Decke kanalisiert. So erreichte der Architekt, dass das Licht, das in die Räume dringt, zum Protagonisten wird und die Essenz der Räume festhält.

The stairs lead to the third floor, which extends horizontally along a space whose contours are blurred.

Les escaliers mènent au troisième étage qui s'étend horizontalement en un espace aux contours estompés.

Die Treppen führen in den dritten Stock, der sich horizontal über einen Raum mit undeffinierten Grenzen erstreckt.

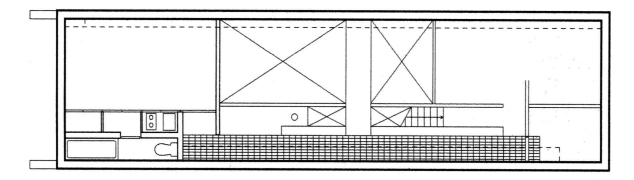

› Plan Plan Grundriss

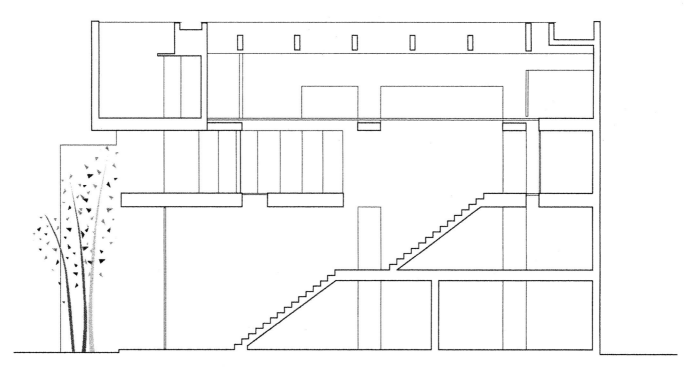

› Section Section Schnitt

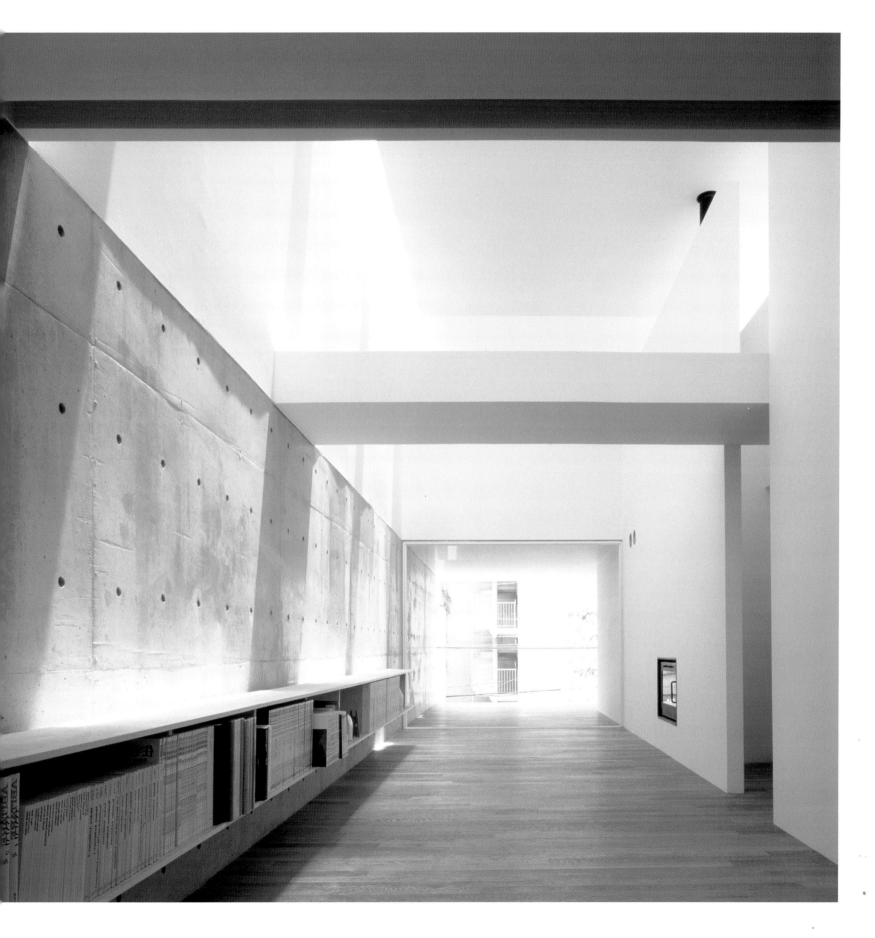

23 House
Maison 23
Haus 23

Salzburg, Austria

Built in the 1930s, this house underwent its first renovation in 1966, when it was divided into three different apartments. In contrst to the original design, the orientation of the interiors has been reworked to take full advantage of the natural light entering each room. In the latest renovation, the architect decided to finish the interiors with a variety of materials to create an interplay of volumes that would have been unthinkable in the original building. The inclination of the ceiling on the upper level creates shadowed areas below, protecting areas like the kitchen and bathroom, which are situated within an open, undefined space.

Construite dans les années 30, l'habitation subit la première restauration en 1966 pour être transformée en trois appartements distincts. A la différence de l'édifice d'origine, l'orientation est aujourd'hui optimalisée pour capter, dans chaque espace, un maximum de lumière naturelle. Lors de cette dernière réhabilitation, l'architecte a décidé d'habiller les intérieurs de divers matériaux qui permettent un jeu de volumes impensable dans le bloc initial. Le toit de bois du niveau supérieur de l'habitation est incliné, générant des zones d'ombre. Les éléments inclus d'ordinaire dans des intérieurs fermés, à l'instar de la salle de bains et de la cuisine, se trouvent ici dans un espace intermédiaire indéfini, protégés par la couverture.

Dieses Haus wurde ca. 1930 errichtet und erstmals 1966 umgebaut, als man drei verschiedene Wohnungen daraus machte. Im Unterschied zum Originalgebäude wurden im Inneren jetzt die Himmelsrichtungen ausgenutzt, um für jeden Raum so viel Licht wie möglich einzufangen. Bei diesem letzten Umbau ließ der Architekt die Räume mit verschiedenen Materialien verkleiden, die ein Spiel mit Formen ermöglichen, das vorher nicht denkbar war. Die Holzdecke im Obergeschoss ist geneigt und schafft schattige Bereiche. Die Wohnbereiche, die sich normalerweise in geschlosenen Räumen befinden, wie z. B. das Bad und die Küche, befinden sich in einem nicht definierten Zwischenraum, beschützt von der Decke.

› Cross section Section transversale Querschnitt

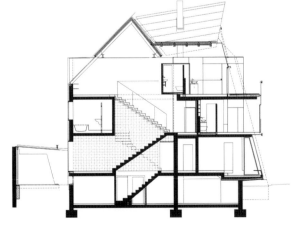

› Longitudinal section Section longitudinale Längsschnitt

House in Madrid
Maison à Madrid
Haus in Madrid

Madrid, Spain

The A-cero studio based the design of this house, on a structure comprising two axes that cross at an oblique angle. The rooms around the first, north-south axis are organized in a series of volumes to form the interior and exterior spaces. The second axis, made up of a portico running from east to west, defines the relationship between the building and the exterior spaces. The slope of the site allows each different level to have an exit to the exterior. The pure lines of this house are reflected in its structural scheme: the intermediate columns were eliminated and replaced by solid reinforced concrete walls and flagstones that trace the contour of the volumes.

Le bureau d'étude « A-cero » a conçu cette maison à partir d'une structure comportant deux axes qui se croisent en formant un angle oblique. Les dépendances s'articulent autour du premier axe, orienté nord-sud, en une série de volumes configurant l'espace intérieur et extérieur. Le second axe, composé d'un portique orienté est-ouest, agence la relation de l'édifice avec les espaces extérieurs de l'habitation. L'inclinaison du terrain permet de doter chaque niveau de sorties vers l'extérieur. La pureté des formes de l'habitation se reflète dans le schéma structurel, abandonnant les piliers intermédiaires pour n'être composé que de murs de béton armé et de dalles dessinant les contours des volumes.

Das Studio A-cero schuf dieses Haus auf Grundlage einer Struktur mit zwei Achsen, die sich in einem schiefen Winkel kreuzen. Um die erste Achse in Nord-Südrichtung liegen die Räume in einer Abfolge von Formen, die einmal innere Räume und einmal Außenanlagen bilden. Die zweite Achse besteht aus einem Säulengang in Ost-West-Richtung. Sie ordnet die Beziehung des Gebäudes zu den äußeren Räumen. Durch die Neigung des Grundstücks konnten in jeder Ebene Türen nach draußen geschaffen werden. Die Reinheit der Formen dieses Hauses spiegelt sich in dem strukturellen Schema wider. Säulen wurden entfernt und die Struktur besteht lediglich aus Mauern aus Stahlbeton und Platten, die den Umriss der Gebäudeteile bilden.

Geometric shapes predominate in the interior, combining perfectly with the natural material chosen.

A l'intérieur, les formes géométriques prédominent, se mariant à merveille avec les matériaux naturels sélectionnés.

Im Inneren herrschen geometrische Formen vor, die perfekt zu den verwendeten natürlichen Materialien passen.

› **Ground floor** Rez-de-chaussée Erdgeschoss

› **First floor** Premier étage Erstes Obergeschoss

› Second floor   Deuxième étage   Zweites Obergeschoss

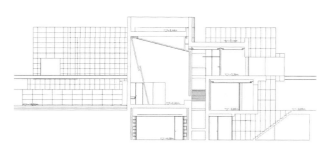

› Section   Section   Schnitt

Shared house
Habitation partagée
Geteiltes Haus

Beijing, China

This aim of this house was to create connections: communication between interior and exterior, between manmade and natural is achieved by means of outdoor spaces such as terraces and courtyards. Furthermore, the relationship between the inhabitants is fomented through communal areas like the dining room and the living room. The building configures the setting through its scale, shape and orientation of its openings – Kanika R'kul offers a prototype of a house whose spatial sequences do not have to be grasped instantaneously. Each place represents an encounter between artificial and natural elements, on different scales and in different proportions. These encounters can be appreciated from different angles, as in the entrance to the courtyard, imbued with a feeling of calm, and the expansive spaces of the dining and living rooms.

Cette habitation essaie d'établir un système de relations : la communication entre l'intérieur et l'extérieur, entre l'homme et la nature, se fait par le biais d'espaces à ciel ouvert, à l'instar de terrasses et de patios et la relation entre les personnes, grâce à des zones communes, comme la salle à manger et le salon. La construction configure le lieu, son échelle, sa forme et l'orientation de ses ouvertures. Kanika R´kul propose des habitations où l'articulation des pièces n'a pas besoin d'être comprise d'emblée. Chaque endroit est un lieu de rencontre entre l'artificiel créé par l'homme et le naturel sous diverses formes et échelles. Il est possible d'apprécier ces différents lieux de rencontre sous diverses perspectives, à l'instar de l'entrée du patio qui transmet un sentiment de tranquillité ou depuis la salle à manger et les salles très spacieuses.

Mit diesem Haus wurde versucht, Verbindungen zu schaffen, eine Kommunikation zwischen innen und außen, zwischen Mensch und Natur. Dies erreichte man durch Räume im Freien wie Terrassen und Höfe und mittels gemeinsamer Bereiche wie dem Speisezimmer und dem Wohnzimmer. Kanika R'kul schuf einen Raum mit einer besonderen Proportion, Form und Richtung der Öffnungen, ein Wohnhaus, dessen Raumsequenzen nicht unbedingt sofort verstanden werden. Jeder Ort stellt ein Aufeinandertreffen des Künstlichen, vom Menschen Geschaffenen, und Natürlichen dar, in verschiedenen Mengen und Größenordnungen. Dieses Aufeinandertreffen kann man aus verschiedenen Winkeln beobachten. Einmal ist da die Ruhe, die der Eingang zum Hof vermittelt oder die Größe des Speisezimmers und Wohnzimmers.

The relationship between the inhabitants is forged through the communal areas, such as the living rooms and the dining room.

La relation entre les personnes est possible grâce aux aires communes, à l'instar des salons et de la salle à manger.

Die Beziehung zwischen den Personen wird durch gemeinsame Bereiche wie Wohnzimmer und Speisezimmer vertieft.

The repetition of colors and shapes endows the space with a minimalist atmosphere.

La répétition des formes et des couleurs imprime l'espace d'une ambiance minimaliste.

Sich wiederholende Farben und Formen lassen den Raum minimalistisch wirken.

White apartment
Appartement blanc
Weißes Appartement

New York, USA

In this project, two older apartments were joined to make a single space. This new space transmits an abstract perception of the interior, reinforced by the elimination of some of the original windows and the use of transparent screens. The client wanted to play with the projection of light on the various planes formed by the ceiling, the walls and the floor. The sliding doors, which stretch from floor to ceiling, appear to float across the floor. The white screens isolate the space from the exterior and contribute to the minimalist esthetic of the apartment. Furthermore, they create an ideal atmposphere for meditation – in clear contrast to the chaos of the world outside. The bright interiors enable the owner to discover and explore new sensations without being overwhelmed by superfluous elements.

Ce projet réunit deux anciens appartements en un seul. Le nouvel espace transmet une perception abstraite de l'intérieur, renforcée par l'élimination de quelques fenêtres d'origines et par l'emploi d'écrans transparents. Le client voulait jouer avec la lumière projetée sur les différents plans formés par le toit, les murs et le sol. Les rails des grandes portes du vestibule sont encastrés et donnent l'impression que les battants glissent sur le sol. Les écrans blancs isolent l'espace de l'extérieur et participent à l'esthétique minimaliste de l'appartement, créant une atmosphère propice à la méditation loin du chaos du monde extérieur. Les intérieurs diaphanes permettent au propriétaire de découvrir et explorer de nouvelles sensations sans être gêné par des éléments superflus.

Zwei Wohnungen wurden zu einer einzigen umgebaut. Die neuen Räumlichkeiten vermitteln eine abstrakte Wahrnehmung des Inneren, die durch die Eliminierung einiger der Originalfenster und die Verwendung transparenter Schirme verstärkt wird. Der Kunde wollte mit dem Einfall des Lichtes auf verschiedene Ebenen, die vom Dach, den Wänden und dem Boden geformt werden, spielen. Die Schienen der vom Boden zur Decke reichenden Türen sind eingelassen, so dass man den Eindruck hat, dass die Türen über den Boden gleiten. Die weißen Schirme trennen die Räume von der Außenwelt ab und leisten ihren Beitrag zur minimalistischen Ästhetik der Wohnung, in der eine meditative Atmosphäre herrscht. Eine Oase, in die man sich von der hektischen Außenwelt zurückziehen kann. Die transparenten Räume lassen die Bewohner neue Empfindungen entdecken, die nicht von überflüssigen Elementen beeinflusst werden.

The transparent white screens isolate the space from the exterior.

Les écrans blancs et translucides isolent l'espace de l'extérieur.

Die weißen, lichtdurchlässigen Schirme isolieren die Räume von der Außenwelt.

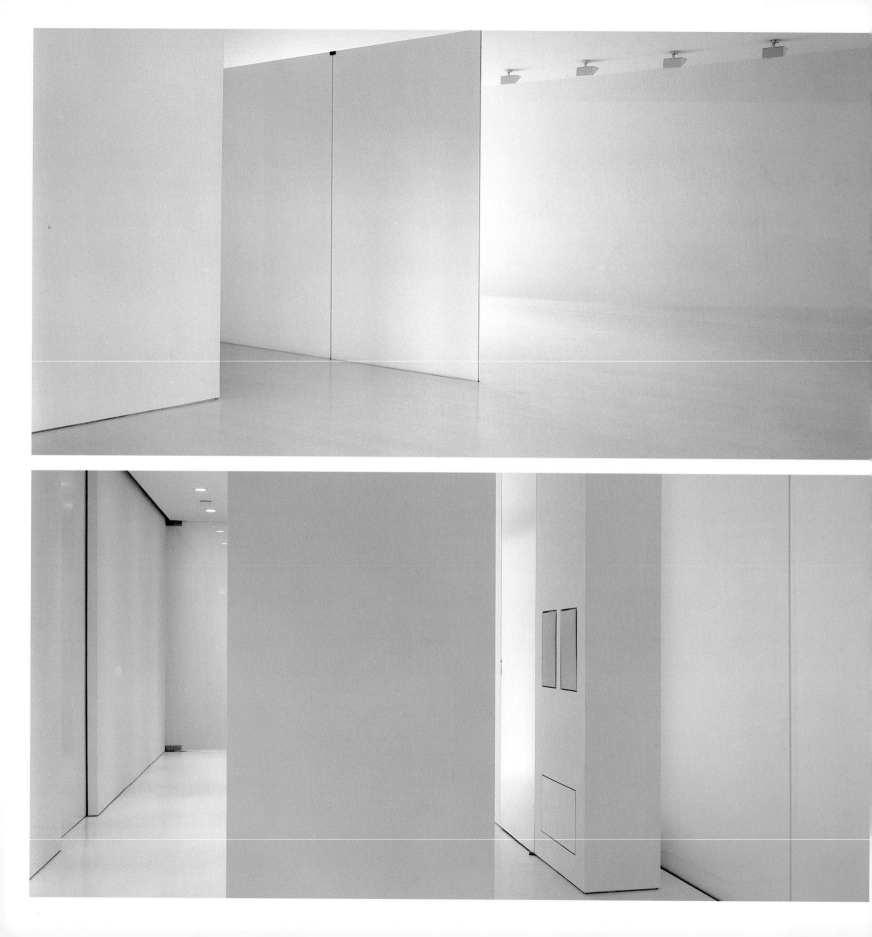

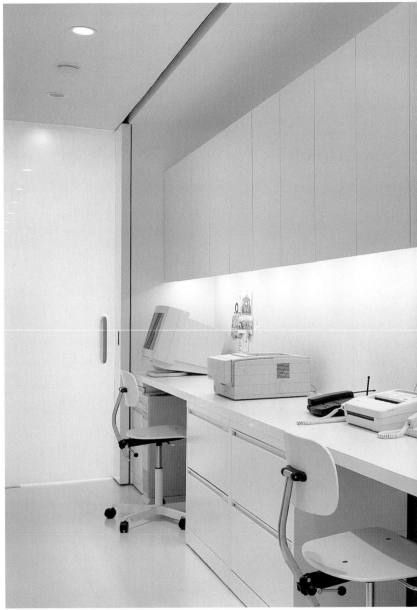

This residence also contains the client's office, which follows the same esthetic lines as the rest of the project.

Le bureau du client est intégré à l'habitat et suit les mêmes lignes esthétiques que le reste du projet.

In der Wohnung befindet sich auch das Büro des Kunden, in dem man den gleichen gestalterischen Richtlinien folgte.

Public Interiors
Intérieurs publics
Öffentliche Interieurs

Deseo Hotel
Hôtel Deseo
Hotel Deseo

Quintana Roo, Mexico

All the rooms in this project look out on to the terrace and pool. The lounge is a relaxing meeting place with views of the huge beds, the jacuzzi and the huge swimming pool. The desire to create a space that would inspire calm and harmony led to this contemporary and peaceful design, in which certain materials and color schemes add a colonial touch. The interior adds to the effect of the architecture with a modernized decor based on ethnic motifs. An example of this essence are the large, comfortable beds located in the outdoor courtyard, where guests can recline under linen canopies that protect one from the sun. The interior rooms keep to the purest of lines, and are based on a minimum of extremely simple elements.

Toutes les pièces de ce projet sont tournées vers la terrasse dotée d'une piscine. Le salon est un lieu de rencontre et de repos où les hôtes peuvent apprécier les immenses lits, le jacuzzi et la piscine. L'idée de concevoir un espace tranquille et harmonieux a donné naissance à ce lieu paisible au design contemporain et agréable, avec des réminiscences d'esprit colonial dans l'emploi de certains matériaux et jeux de couleurs. L'intérieur exalte les lignes architecturales grâce à un mobilier d'inspiration à la fois ethnique et contemporain. Cet esprit est présent dans les grands lits confortables du patio extérieur, installés sous des vélums de lin qui les protégent du soleil. Les pièces intérieures suivent une ligne claire basée sur un minimum d'éléments très simples.

Alle Räume des Hotels liegen zur Terrasse mit Swimmingpool. Die Lounge ist Treffpunkt oder ein Ort der Entspannung, wo die Gäste die riesigen Liegen, den Whirlpool und den Swimmingpool genießen können. Es wurde ein Ort voller Ruhe und Harmonie geschaffen, im zeitgenössischen und gelassenen Design, mit einem leichten Anklang von Kolonialstil durch die verwendeten Materialien und Farbspiele. In den Räumen werden die architektonischen Linien noch durch ein ethnisch inspiriertes, aber modernes Mobiliar unterstrichen. Ein Beispiel dafür sind die großen, bequemen Liegen im Hof im Freien, die mit schattenspendenen Leinenstoffen überspannt sind. Die inneren Räume sind ebenfalls in sehr reinen Linien gehalten und mit wenigen, sehr einfachen Elementen ausgestattet.

Outside, the large beds and linen canopies endow the lounge with the required peace and calm.

A l'extérieur, les grands lits sous les vélums de lin apportent le calme et la détente nécessaires.

Draußen stehen große Liegen mit Sonnendächern aus Leinen. Hier können die Gäste Ruhe und Entspannung finden.

Marco Savorelli

325

Brescia, Italy

Bar in Brescia
Bar à Brescia
Bar in Brescia

This minimalist locale, setting northern Italy is characterized by a sober design and lighting that takes advantage of the limited range of colors used in the decor. The space unfolds on an a open plane predominated by horizontal lines, while the leather furniture and sophisticated system of halogen lighting further contribute to the evocative effect. The mirrors on the walls seem to dramatically increase the real dimensions of the space and amplify the purity of the lines and the serenity of the gray decor. The designers opted for soft lighting, which can be discerned between the lines of the structure. The result is a relaxed and pleasant atmosphere, an ideal place to unwind.

Cet établissement minimaliste, situé au nord de l'Italie, est défini par la sobriété de son design et par un éclairage qui optimise la palette réduite de couleurs employées dans la décoration. L'espace se déroule selon un plan ouvert où l'horizontalité prédomine. Le revêtement en cuir du mobilier et un système sophistiqué d'éclairage halogène contribuent à créer un effet suggestif. Les miroirs au mur augmentent de manière significative les dimensions réelles de l'espace, exaltant la pureté des lignes et la sérénité qui se dégage des tons gris tout en élégance. L'éclairage tamisé, se devine entre les profils de la structure. Cette option permet d'obtenir une ambiance détendue et agréable, idéale pour les réunions entre amis.

Dieses minimalistisch gestaltete Lokal in Norditalien zeichnet sich durch seine schlichte Gestaltung und die Beleuchtung aus. Nur wenig Farben wurden bei der Dekoration verwendet. Der Raum liegt auf einer offenen Ebene, auf der die waagerechten Linien vorherrschen. Die Möbel sind mit Leder überzogen und ein ausgeklügeltes System mit Hallogenleuchten lässt die Räume sehr ansprechend wirken. Die Spiegel an den Wänden lassen den Raum optisch größer wirken, und sie vervielfältigen die Reinheit der Linien und die Gelassenheit der eleganten Grautöne. Die sanfte Beleuchtung kann zwischen den Profilen der Struktur nur erraten werden. So entstand eine entspannte und angenehme Atmosphäre, ideal für freundschaftliche Zusammenkünfte.

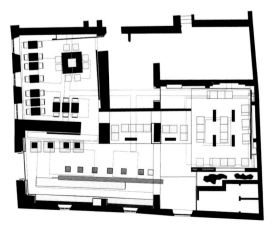

› Plan Plan Grundriss

St. Paul Hotel
Hôtel St. Paul
Hotel St. Paul

Montreal, Canada

This space is defined by its contrasting elements, reflected, for example, in the juxtaposition between its classical exterior and contemporary interior, or the impact of chiaroscuro on its decor. The initial proposal was an irresistible commission for the architect who designed the hotel: she was to achieve a harmonic ensemble based on elements that would seemingly be antagonistic. The openness of the spaces lent itself to the creation of bright rooms, whose dynamic nature was emphasized using suggestive and intense colors. As for the furnishings, the architect chose pieces with well-conceived geometrical designs, whose decorative details accentuate the explosion of color in the interior and hint at long-lost luxury and splendor.

Le design de cet espace est déterminé par le contraste qui se reflète, par exemple, dans la juxtaposition du style classique de l'extérieur et l'intérieur contemporain ou dans les effets intéressants créés par le jeu de clair-obscur. L'architecte s'est passionné pour la proposition initiale, à savoir obtenir un ensemble harmonieux à partir d'éléments antagonistes. La générosité des espaces se prête à la création de pièces diaphanes dont le dynamisme est sublimé par l'emploi de couleurs et de teintes intenses et suggestives. Quant au mobilier, le choix s'est porté sur des designs aux géométries exquises, avec des détails de décoration accentuant l'explosion des couleurs des intérieurs où l'on devine des réminiscences de luxe et de la splendeur d'époques révolues.

Das definierende Element der Raumgestaltung dieses Hotels ist der Kontrast, den man zum Beispiel in der Gegenüberstellung des klassischen Stils der Fassade und der zeitgenössischen Ausstattung im Inneren erkennen kann, oder an den auffallenden Effekten des Spiels mit Hell und Dunkel. Die Zielvorgabe der Kunden war eine unwiderstehliche Herausforderung an die Architekten. Es sollte ein harmonisches Ganzes aus gegensätzlichen Elementen entstehen. Die weiten Räumen eigneten sich gut zur Schaffung offener Umgebungen, deren Dynamik duch die intensiven und ansprechenden Farben unterstrichen wurde. Man wählte Möbel mit einer edlen Geometrie und Dekorationselemente, die die Farbexplosion in den Räumen noch unterstreichen. Anspielungen auf vergangene Epochen voller Luxus und Pracht.

The spaces used as communal areas both expansive and open. They are dominated by chiaroscuro elements and geometrical forms.

Les espaces réservés aux aires communes, généreux et ouverts, sont dominés par les clairs-obscurs et la géométrie des formes.

Die Gemeinschaftsbereiche sind großzügig und offen angelegt und werden von dem Spiel mit dem Helldunkel und der Geometrie der Formen dominiert.

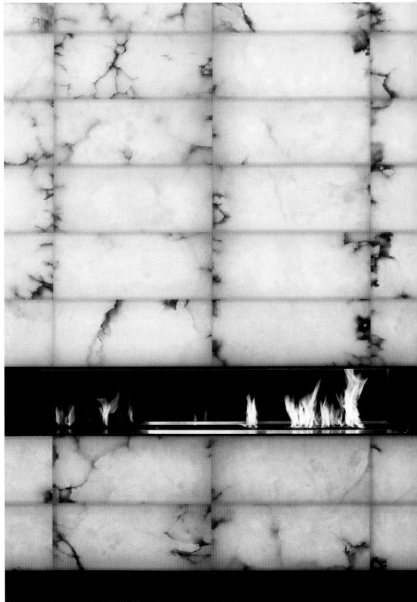

334

Bed Supperclub

Bangkok, Thailand

This brilliantly modern restaurant and bar is located within an enormous, futuristic steel tube. Consisting of two levels aligned on either side of the tube, the pure forms of this space are complemented by sofas and beds with a smattering of cushions, as well as a highly original decor. The white walls serve as a screen on which a computerized lighting system projects changing combinations of colors all night long. During the day, the light penetrating the large glass structure at one end of the tube gives the setting an ethereal quality, with diffuse, neutral interior enveloped in white. It comes as no surprise that this establishment has quickly become one of the most popular meeting places in the city.

Ce refuge superbe et moderne pour dîner et se relaxer s'inscrit au cœur d'un énorme tube d'acier futuriste. Constitué de deux niveaux alignés de chaque côté du tube, cet espace aux formes pures est meublé de sofas et de lits émaillés de coussins et de détails décoratifs originaux. Le blanc des murs provient d'un écran où un système d'éclairage électronique projette, la nuit, des combinaisons changeantes de couleurs. Pendant la journée, la lumière qui pénètre la grande structure de verre, depuis l'une des extrémités du tube, métamorphose l'établissement en une unité éthérée où le blanc habille un intérieur diffus et neutre. Il n'est pas étonnant que cet établissement soit devenu un des lieux de réunion les plus courus de la ville.

Dieser moderne und perfekte Zufluchtsort zum Abendessen oder zur Entspannung befindet sich in einem futuristischen, riesigen Stahlrohr. Das Lokal hat zwei Ebenen, die linear auf den beiden Seiten des Rohres verlaufen. Dieser Raum mit seinen reinen Formen ist mit Sofas und Liegen voller Kissen und origineller Dekorationselemente ausgestattet. Das Weiß der Wände wirkt wie ein Schirm, auf den ein Beleuchtungssystem nachts verschiedene Farbkombinationen projiziert. Tagsüber dringt das Licht durch eine große Glasstruktur an einem Ende des Rohres ein. Hier, wo die Farbe Weiß das Innere verschwimmen lässt und neutralisiert, wirkt das Lokal ätherisch. So ist es nicht erstaunlich, dass dieses Lokal zu einem der beliebtesten Treffpunkte der Stadt wurde.

The concepts of bar and restaurant are fused together in this space to form ethereal, intimate canvas designed by Orbit Studio.

Le bar et le restaurant fusionnent dans ce lieu, transformé en une grande toile de fond éthérée et intime par le bureau Orbit Studio.

Die Bar und das Restaurant vermischen sich. Es entsteht eine große, ätherische und intimistische Leinwand, ein Werk von Orbit Studio.

Convent de la Missió Hotel
Hôtel Convent de la Missió
Convent de la Missió Hotel

Palma de Mallorca, Spain

This client required a simple yet elegant home that would respond to his needs as well as his passion for Zen philosophy, based on contemplation and meditation. The architects worked from this brief, and – taking advantage of a truly remarkable site – designed a restrained interior whose soft colors combine with discreetly elegant, sleek furnishings. The space was distributed rationally to take advantage of the exceptional views. In the interior, the perfect combination of materials and textures takes on special importance, resulting in a delicate, quiet atmosphere. Neutral tones, in an interior that mostly eschews dark colors, are another of the keys to this project.

Le client voulait une habitation au design simple et élégant qui corresponde à ses besoins et à sa passion pour la philosophie zen basée sur la contemplation et la méditation. Les architectes sont partis de ce programme et, profitant de la situation splendide de l'habitation, ont conçu un intérieur discret, aux tons doux, doté d'un mobilier aux lignes pures et d'une élégance subtile. L'espace suit une organisation rationnelle afin de pouvoir jouir des vues exceptionnelles. A l'intérieur, les matériaux et les textures revêtent une importance toute particulière et leur mariage parfait crée une ambiance feutrée, emprunte de subtilité. Les tons neutres, dans un intérieur où les couleurs sombres sont à peine présentes, sont une des clés de voûte de ce projet.

Der Kunde wünschte sich ein einfach und elegant gestaltetes Haus, das seine Anforderungen erfüllt und seiner Neigung zur Zen-Philosophie, die auf der Betrachtung und Meditation basiert, entspricht. Diese Kundenwünsche bildeten die Grundlage der Planung und die Architekten nutzten die wundervolle Lage des Hauses, um zurückhaltende Räumlichkeiten in sanften Tönen zu entwerfen, ausgestattet mit Möbeln in reinen Linien voller diskreter Eleganz. Der Raum wurde rational organisiert, so dass man den wundervollen Blick genießen kann. Man richtete einen besonderen Augenmerk auf die Materialien und Texturen, die in den Räumen verwendet wurden. Durch die perfekte Kombination entstand eine wohnliche und feine Atmosphäre. Die neutralen Farben im Inneren prägen den Charakter der Räume.

The homogeneous textures and uniform finishes blur the defining lines of the living room.

L'homogénéité des textures et l'uniformité des finitions gomment les limites du salon.

Die Homogenität der Texturen und die Einheitlichkeit der Flächen radieren die Begrenzungen des Wohnzimmers aus.

The fireplace, built into the wall in one of the quietest parts of the house, stands out from the linear shapes of the walls.

Dans l'une des pièces les plus retirées de la maison, la cheminée, encastrée dans un mur aux formes linéaires, se détache, à l'instar d'une sculpture.

In einem der wohnlichsten Winkel des Hauses befindet sich ein skulptureller Kamin, der in eine Wand mit linearen Formen eingelassen ist.

White plays an important role throughout, while the neutral and diffuse lighting creates a relaxed and intimate interior.

Le blanc est le protagoniste de toutes les pièces. L'éclairage neutre et diffus crée un intérieur qui décline détente et intimité.

Die Farbe Weiß beherrscht die Räume. Durch die neutrale und gedämpfte Beleuchtung entstand eine entspannte und intime Atmosphäre.

Mojiko Hotel
Hôtel Mojiko
Hotel Mojiko

Fukuoka, Japan

The exterior of this building, which resembles a boat, looks out over the straits of Kanmon and blends into the serene landscape. The classic, homely bars of yesteryear were the inspiration behind the interior, though the materials used add a dash of seductiveness and complicity: the result is a warm and poetic space that invites both conversation and relaxation. The structure of the unique lighting system comprises a network of iron bars suspended from the ceiling; the individual lights hang from it and can be positioned to suit one's tastes. The private rooms bespeak the exquisite touch of Minimalism in its purest form, rejecting redundant or unnecessary details in favor of simplicity.

L'extérieur de cet édifice, qui s'assimile à la structure d'un bateau, fait face au détroit de Kanmon et se fond au paysage paisible. Ses intérieurs s'inspirent d'un bar traditionnel et agréable d'autrefois mais les matériaux utilisés dotent l'ensemble d'une pointe de séduction et de complicité créant un espace chaleureux et poétique qui invite à dialoguer et à se reposer. L'armature du système d'éclairage original est formée d'un treillis de barres de fer suspendues au toit, soutenant les sources de lumière orientables. Les espaces de vie privés subliment l'élégance exquise du minimalisme le plus pur qui fuit les détails superflus et inutiles pour ne parler que le langage de la simplicité.

Dieses Gebäude, das in seiner Struktur einem Schiff gleicht, liegt zur Kanmon-Meerenge und verschmilzt mit der idyllischen Landschaft. Die Raumgestaltung wird von einer klassischen und freundlichen alten Bar inspiriert. Die verwendeten Materialien fügen dem Gesamtbild einen Touch von Verführung und Konspiration bei, so dass ein warmer und poetischer Raum entstand, der zu einem netten Gespräch und zur Entspannung einlädt. Das Originalgerüst der Beleuchtung besteht aus einer Struktur aus Eisenstangen, die an der Decke hängt und an der drehbare Beleuchtungskörper hängen. Die privaten Räume zeigen sich im edelsten minimalistischen Design, das überflüssige und unnötige Einzelheiten vermeidet und die Sprache der Einfachheit spricht.

Ridaura Civic Center
Centre civique de Ridaura
Bürgerzentrum in Ridaura

Girona, Spain

The challenge of this project consisted in designing a flexible civic center that could be used for a wide variety of activities. The building is small in size and stretches transversally across the site. This freed the area in front of the main entrance for use as a square. In the back, a larger space is given over to games, dancing and sport. The outdoor spaces are connected by means of a series of porches, while skylights, platforms and belvederes lend form to a structure capable of housing a diverse range of activities. The distinctiveness of the Ridaura Civic Center lies in its modern design, which contrasts with its rural surroundings.

Ce projet devait relever le défi de concevoir un centre civique modulable qui puisse accueillir diverses activités. L'édifice aux dimensions réduites a été implanté transversalement sur le terrain prévu afin de libérer une aire, face à l'entrée principale, qui puisse se convertir en une place. Sur l'arrière, une zone plus large est réservée aux jeux, danses et sports. La relation entre les espaces à l'air libre s'établit grâce à une série de porches, tandis que velux, plates-formes et miradors forment une structure capable d'accueillir des activités diverses. La particularité du Centre Civique de Ridaura repose sur la modernité de son design qui contraste avec l'environnement rural où il se trouve.

Die Herausforderung bei dieser Planung bestand darin, ein Bürgerzentrum zu schaffen, das verschiedenen Zwecken dienen sollte. Das Gebäude ist nicht besonders groß und wurde quer auf das zur Verfügung stehende Grundstück gebaut, damit etwas Freiraum vor dem Haupteingang bleibt, auf dem ein Platz angelegt werden sollte. Im hinteren, geräumigeren Teil sollten Spiele, Tanz und Sport stattfinden. Durch eine Reihe von Vorhallen, entsand eine Verbindung der Räume im Freien Dachfenster, Plattformen und Aussichtspunkte schaffen eine Struktur, die sich für verschiedene Arten von Aktivitäten eignet. Was das Bürgerzentrum Ridaura so einzigartig macht, ist die moderne Gestaltung, die zu der ländlichen Umgebung, in der es sich befindet, einen großen Gegensatz bildet.

The horizontal parallelepiped that makes up the house contrasts with the verticality of the nearby church.

Le parallélépipède horizontal formé par l'édifice contraste avec la verticalité de l'église proche.

Das waagerechte Parallelepipedum des Gebäudes steht im Gegensatz zu der Vertikalität der nahe gelegenen Kirche.

The glass enclosures and skylights fill the interior with abundant natural light.

Les portes et baies vitrées ainsi que les velux laissent la lumière naturelle entrer à flots et fluctuer vers les espaces intérieurs.

Die verglasten Wände und die Dachfenster lassen reichlich Tageslicht in alle Räume einfallen.

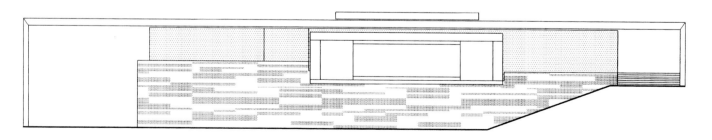

› Section Section Schnitt

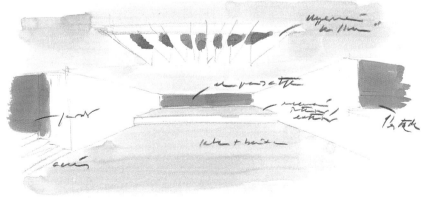

Miami Beach, USA

The Shore Club

The atmosphere in this space transmits a sensation of lightness thanks to the use of pale colors. The illuminated backdrops and other elements – such as the oriental candles – create a setting that encourages meditation or relaxation. Furthermore, the polished surfaces and absence of distracting details highlight the geometry of the structural elements. The decor – typified by straight lines – contrasts with the sinuous stairway that leads to the upper levels, whose stone treads are enveloped by a white structure reminiscent of papyrus plants. The space was designed to maximize exterior lighting throughout this intimate relationship with the exterior is achieved through a number of courtyards that are highly propitious to relaxation.

L'atmosphère de cet espace transmet une sensation de légèreté grâce à l'emploi de tons clairs. Les rideaux éclairés à l'arrière et certains éléments comme les chandeliers au style oriental, s'inscrivent dans une mise en scène qui invite à la méditation et à la détente. Les surfaces polies et l'absence de détails qui obstruent la vue, exaltent la géométrie des éléments structurels. Le mobilier, aux lignes droites, contraste avec les sinuosités de l'escalier qui mène aux niveaux supérieurs. Les marches en pierre se cachent sous une structure enveloppante blanche rappelant un papyrus. L'espace a été prévu pour bénéficier à tout instant de l'éclairage extérieur. Ce lien étroit avec l'extérieur est possible grâce aux nombreux patios qui invitent au repos.

Die Atmosphäre in diesen Räumen vermittelt einen Eindruck von Leichtigkeit, bedingt durch die hellen Farben, die verwendet wurden. Die beleuchteten Vorhänge im Hintergrund und Elemente wie orientalische Kerzen schaffen eine Umgebung, die zur Meditation und zum Entspannen einlädt. Die polierten Oberflächen und das Fehlen von Elementen, die den Blick behindern, heben die Geometrie der Strukturelemente noch hervor. Die geradlinigen Möbel stehen im kontrast zu der kurvigen Treppe, die nach oben führt. Die Steinstufen sind unter einer weißen Umhüllung versteckt, die an Papyrus erinnert. Das Licht von draußen wird in diesen Räumen zu jeder Tageszeit ausgenutzt. Durch zahlreiche Höfe, die zum Ausruhen eingeladen, entstand eine enge Beziehung zu Außenwelt.

The treads of the stairs are enveloped by a sinuous structure reminiscent of papyrus.

Les marches se cachent sous une structure sinueuse qui rappelle celle des papyrus.

Die Stufen sind unter einer kurvigen Struktur verborgen, die an Papyrus erinnert.

Shanghai, China

Spa Evian

This spa is located on the second and third floor of the building Three on the Bund, located in the center of Shanghai. The objective here was to materialize the purity associated with the Evian brand, as well as to emphasize concepts such as transparency and calm. The project also foresaw the integration of an existing entrance hall, which was incorporated as a garden. The atmosphere in the various rooms was achieved through the use of delicate, liquid textures on the walls and soft lighting, instilling spa with the required peace and calm. Spatial integrity and impeccable details lend a special seductiveness to each room. In the middle of the central hall, a stairway with a glass banister reaches to the second floor; from here, the treads of the staircase reflect the geometric purity characteristic of the entire project.

Cette station thermale se trouve aux deuxième et troisième étages de l'édifice « Three on the Bund », dans le centre populaire de la ville. L'objectif était de matérialiser la pureté liée à la marque Evian et de mettre l'accent sur certains concepts comme la transparence et le calme. En outre, le projet prévoyait d'intégrer le vestibule existant à la manière d'un jardin. L'atmosphère des différents espaces de vie est créée à partir de textures aqueuses délicates recouvrant les murs et grâce à un éclairage doux qui suggère le calme désiré. L'intégrité spatiale et l'amour des détails dotent chaque pièce d'un charme particulier. Au cœur du vestibule central, des escaliers aux rambardes de verre s'élèvent vers le deuxième étage. De cette perspective, les marches sont empreintes de la pureté géométrique qui caractérise tout l'ensemble.

Dieses Heilbad befindet sich in der zweiten und dritten Etage des bekannten Gebäudes „Three on the Bund" im Zentrum der Stadt. Die Architekten hatten es sich zum Ziel gesetzt, die Reinheit, die die Marke Evian symbolisiert, umzusetzen und Konzepte wie Transparenz und Ruhe zu unterstreichen. Außerdem sollte die bereits vorhandene Vorhalle in die Planung miteinbezogen werden, und so machte man eine Art Garten daraus. Die ruhige Atomsphäre in den verschiedenen Räumen wird durch zierliche, wässrige Texturen an den Wänden und eine angenehme, indirekte Beleuchtung unterstrichen. Die räumliche Einheitlichkeit und die Klarheit der Details unterstreichen die besondere Wirkung jedes Raums. In der Mitte des zentralen Vestibüls führt eine Treppe mit gläsernem Geländer in den zweiten Stock. Von hier aus betrachtet besitzen die Treppenstufen die geometrische Reinheit, die die gesamte Gestaltung kennzeichnet.

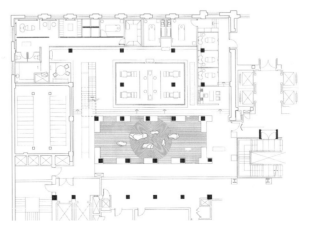

› **First floor** Premier étage Erstes Obergeschoss

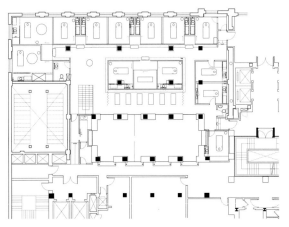

› Second floor   Deuxième étage   Zweites Obergeschoss

Mandarin Oriental Hotel
Hôtel Mandarin Oriental
Hotel Mandarin Oriental

Miami, USA

This building presents a resplendent appearance throughout thanks to a series of large windows in the foyer that flood it with natural light. The interior unfolds through a continuous interplay between horizontal and vertical planes, which give rise to a landscape that is simultaneously both broken and fluid. The architects proposed a space of comfortable proportions with extremely high ceilings, in order to create an uncluttered and expansive layout. The majestic marble columns that preside over the foyer blend in perfectly with the exalted character of the building, while the exuberant plantings and colorful furnishings accentuate the tropical ambience of the hotel's public spaces. The large windows guarantee a dialogue with the exterior at all times.

Cet édifice présente à tout instant une image resplendissante grâce à sa structure qui permet à la lumière d'entrer à flots à travers les larges baies vitrées du vestibule. L'intérieur se déploie dans un échange continu de plans horizontaux et verticaux qui crée un paysage accidenté et fluide. Les architectes ont proposé un vaste espace, aux toits élancés, pour créer une distribution intérieure claire et vaste. Les colonnes majestueuses de marbre qui mènent au hall d'entrée s'intègrent à merveille au caractère sublime de tout l'ensemble. La végétation exubérante et les coloris du mobilier exaltent l'ambiance tropicale des espaces communs. Les grandes baies vitrées permettent à tout moment un dialogue avec l'extérieur.

Dieses Gebäude wirkt aufgrund seiner Struktur, die reichlich Tageslicht durch die großen Fenster im Vestibül einströmen lässt, sehr klar. Im Inneren wechseln sich waagerechte Ebenen mit senkrechten ab, so dass eine gebrochene, doch flüssige Landschaft entsteht. Die Architekten schufen einen großen Raum mit sehr hohen Decken, um die innere Aufteilung klar und frei wirken zu lassen. Die majestätischen Marmorsäulen in der Eingangshalle fügen sich perfekt in das erhabene Gesamtbild des Hotels ein. Die üppigen Pflanzen und die bunten Möbel unterstreichen die tropische Atmosphäre in den öffentlich zugänglichen Räumen. Die großen Fenster ermöglichen einen ständigen Dialog mit der Außenwelt.

The light that enters through the large windows in the foyer highlights the hotel's bright, majestic character.

La lumière qui pénètre par les grandes baies vitrées du vestibule exalte le caractère diaphane et majestueux de l'hôtel.

Das Licht, das durch die großen Fenster im Vestibül fällt, unterstreicht den offenen und majestätischen Charakter des Hotels.

One of the most important – and attractive – spaces in the hotel is this oriental-style meeting area, which encourages meditation.

Un des espaces principaux les plus aimés, est ce point de rencontre au style oriental qui invite à la méditation.

Einer der wichtigsten und beliebtesten Räume ist der Treffpunkt im orientalischen Stil, der zur Meditation einlädt.

One of the main objectives was to preserve the equilibrium and purity of the private rooms.

L'un des objectifs principaux est de préserver l'équilibre et la pureté des espaces de vie à usage privé.

Eines der wichtigsten Planungsziele war es, das Gleichgewicht und die Reinheit der Räume zu wahren.

Straf Hotel
Hôtel Straf
Hotel Straf

Milan, Italy

In designing this hotel, the architect sought a fluid and cosmopolitan interior. Accordingly he chose materials like iron, cement, slate, acid-treated mirrors, polished brass and crepe, and then combined them with glass panels to create an effect of transparency. The result is without parallel. This daring proposal, based on an intriguing language of contrasts and textures, unfolds in a space built under the watchful eye of the architect. A rational and ordered interior was achieved through the careful treatment of details and refined taste in the selection of structural materials. In the rooms, endowed with a warm minimalism, materials take precedence over details. There are no elements to imped an overall view of the ensemble, and the various components hark back to a classical past that has still not completely disappeared.

L'architecte voulait créer un intérieur fluide et cosmopolite. A cet effet, il a sélectionné des matériaux comme le fer, le ciment, l'ardoise, les miroirs traités à l'acide, le laiton lustré ou le crêpe qu'il a mélangés à des panneaux de verre pour obtenir un effet de transparence. Le résultat est unique. Le projet audacieux, basé sur un langage intéressant de contrastes et de textures, débouche sur un espace érigé sous la surveillance étroite de l'architecte. Le traitement peaufiné des détails et la sélection épurée des matériaux structuraux ont donné naissance à un intérieur rationnel et clair. Dans les pièces à vivre, d'un minimalisme chaleureux, les matériaux sont plus importants que les détails. Aucun élément n'entrave la vision de l'ensemble et les différentes composantes évoquent un passé classique qui n'a pas encore disparu.

Der Architekt schuf eine fließende und kosmopolitische Atmosphäre. Dazu wählte er Materialien wie Eisen, Zement, Schiefer, mit Säure behandelte Spiegel, poliertes Messing und sogar Gaze zwischen Glasscheiben, um die Räume transparent wirken zu lassen. Das Ergebnis entstand unter der strengen Überwachung des Architekten, und durch seinen gewagten Vorschlag, der auf einer interessanten Sprache aus Kontrasten und Texturen beruht. Alle Einzelheiten sind sehr sorgfältig bearbeitet und die Strukturmaterialien perfekt ausgewählt, so dass die Räume rational und geordnet wirken. Die Zimmer sind von einem warmen Minimalismus geprägt, die Materialien sind wichtiger als die Details. Kein Element behindert die Sicht auf das Ganze und verschiedene Elemente erinnern an die klassische Vergangenheit, die noch nicht vollständig verschwunden ist.

The rooms echo a classical rationalism based on clean lines and details.

Les pièces se réfèrent au rationalisme classique fondé sur la pureté des lignes et des détails.

Die Zimmer sind in einer Art klassischem Rationalismus gestaltet, der auf der Reinheit der Linien und Details beruht.

The updated, cosmopolitan vocabulary gives rise to contemporary details, such as the photographs displayed on one of the walls.

Un langage rénové et cosmopolite offre des détails contemporains à l'instar de la photographie exposée sur l'un des murs.

Eine neue und kosmopolitische Sprache leistet ihren Beitrag mit Einzelheiten wie den Fotografien, die an den Wänden ausgestellt werden.

Photo Credits Crédits photographiques Fotonachweis